Roger W. M

with Print and Rowbotham

Managerial Finance,

Shareholder Value

and Value Based Management

Linking Business Performance and Value Creation

Design and Typesetting: Mars Business Associates Ltd

Printed and bound in Great Britain by: Butler and Tanner Ltd

Reprinted: June 2001, April 2003

LIBRARY OF CONGRESS CATALOGING IN PUBLICATION DATA

Mills, Roger W.

Managerial Finance, Shareholder Value and Value Based Management

Roger W. Mills   with Carole F. Print and Sean A. Rowbotham

Included bibliographies and index

ISBN   1 873186 11 8

1. Finance, Strategy

I. Title

Publisher:
Mars Business Associates Ltd., 62 Kingsmead, Lechlade, Glos. GL7 3BW
Tel/Fax: +44 1367 252506   Email: john@marspub.co.uk

Author:
Roger W. Mills
Tel: 07071 888888   Email: DrRWMills@aol.com

About the author

Roger W. Mills B.Tech (Hons), MSc., Phd., is Professor of Accounting and Finance at Henley Management College and is also a Consultant Professor on Shareholder Value to PricewaterhouseCoopers. He is a Fellow of the Chartered Institute of Management Accountants the Chartered Institute of Secretaries and Administrators and the Association of Corporate Treasurers. His key research, teaching and consulting areas are shareholder, strategic and business valuation; financial aspects of strategy; corporate performance appraisal techniques; applied corporate finance. He is the author of books entitled: The Dynamics of Shareholder Value and Strategic Value Analysis. Roger has written numerous articles and he has extensive international experience particularly in Europe, the US, the Asia Pacific Region and South America and has also worked in Europe, Central and Southern Africa and the US.

with

Carole F. Print, D.B.A., is a member of the Faculty at Henley Management College where she teaches accounting and finance, primarily on the taught MBA programmes. She is an Associate member of the Chartered Institute of Management Accountants and spent her early career in industry, working in both financial and management accounting. She has been involved in management education since the early 1980's. Carole completed her Doctor of Business Administration degree in 1999 in which she undertook exploratory research into the implementation of shareholder value.

and

Sean A. Rowbotham, BSc., M.B.A., is an Assistant Director within the Financial Strategy service line of Ernst and Young's Corporate Finance practice in London. He is a Fellow of the Institute of Chartered Accountants, an Associate of the Royal College of Science and holds the Diploma in Marketing from the Chartered Institute of Marketing. Sean has held senior roles within finance and strategic planning in a number of global corporations including Dow Jones Corporation, Swiss Re and British Telecommunications plc.

Acknowledgements

It is rare for a book to be the product of a single person's endeavours. Like a stage production, many work behind the scenes to help those in the limelight deliver on the day. This book was no exception.

I should like to thank the many individuals who assisted me in the writing of the book for their helpful suggestions. As always, any errors which remain are mine!

Preface

The business world of today is turbulent and organisations of all types have to make choices about how to manage scarce resources in a climate so often characterised by considerable and rapid change. Increasingly organisations are embracing the principles of shareholder value as a key business objective and many have gone even further in implementing what has come to be known as Value Based Management, or VBM for short. VBM has profound implications for all functional areas of the business, not least of which is the finance function.

There are different views about what actually constitutes VBM and how to implement it. In this book we review VBM within the context of a changing world for the finance function. We review and illustrate the principles upon which shareholder value is based and discuss the alternative approaches that may be used to measure and guide value creation. We also provide our view on how VBM can be implemented and its relationship with approaches like the Balanced Scorecard and Business Excellence Model. The truth of the matter is that VBM implementation is tough and if it is to be taken down into the business as a whole, the adoption of approaches like the Balanced Scorecard and the Business Excellence Model is essential.

Our experience has provided us with insights about how procedurally VBM implementation can be best achieved and we summarise this within a 10-step approach. It is by no means the only approach, but it is that which we have found to work well in organisations of various types and sizes. Last, but not least, we draw upon the research of a member of our team that was undertaken over a 5 year period and which studied the implementation of shareholder value within three large companies.

Roger W. Mills   August 1999

Contents

Chapter 4: Assessing Competitive Advantage

Chapter 5: Terminal Value and the Cost of Capital

Chapter 6: Business Value, Economic Profit and Performance Measurement

Chapter 7: Value Based Management Implementation

Chapter 8: Implementing VBM – The Evidence

Chapter 1

Shareholder Value, Value Creation and Financial Management

Chapter Preview

- Shareholder value as a key objective.

- New metrics associated with the drive towards shareholder value.

- The move from traditional accounting measures to the new shareholder based metrics.

- Momentum behind shareholder value developments in Europe.

- Link between shareholder value and financial management.

- The changing role of the financial specialist.

- The ascendancy of the 'general financial manager.'

The drive to create shareholder value

Since the 1980's, the objective of creating 'shareholder value' by earning an economic return on capital invested in excess of the cost of that capital, has spread from the US and has been adopted increasingly by companies. A number of shareholder value approaches have emerged, which draw upon the financial theory of value, which is that value in economic terms being considered as the present value of the firm's expected future net cash flows.

Major US companies like *Coca–Cola, Westinghouse, Quaker Oats* have been promoting the creation of value for their shareholders, and many companies in the UK now incorporate some form of mission statement concerning the maximisation or creation of shareholder value as being their prime corporate objective. The acceptance in the UK of firstly, a cash flow approach to measuring shareholder value, and secondly the adoption of the view that maximising shareholder value is maximising the firm's current market value have been developments during the late 1980 and 1990s.

The acceptance of cash flow approaches to valuation has been accompanied by a trend to place less importance on traditional accounting measures such as earnings per share, and has seen the evolution and development of a number of new methods, or metrics, for measuring company performance. These new metrics all share the same basic premise that a company only creates value if the economic return on its capital is greater than the cost of that capital. Different metrics have been, and are being, developed and promoted by consultants, which adopt slightly different approaches to maximising shareholder value. These can be summarised under the following three groupings, and will be considered in *Chapters 3 and 6*.

1. Free cash flow

At its simplest, the basic free cash flow model uses a framework of generic value drivers to provide a view of the present value of cash available to the providers of finance, both equity and debt, over the future time period in which there is considered to be competitive advantage. Such free cash flows include investments in whatever form to support the existing and future business, but exclude any financing costs. Any financing costs are included when measuring the cost of capital, which is used as the rate at which to discount the free cash flows to a present value. This present value represents the value of the business as a whole and needs to be adjusted for the impact of any external investments and debt to convert it to the value of the equity. When divided by the number of ordinary shares, this gives an estimate of the value per share which, for a publicly traded company, can be compared with its share price.

In some cases, like banks and financial institutions, such an approach may be inappropriate for a number of reasons. For example, the cash inflow of a bank arises from interest and banks do not have debt in the traditional sense of a non–regulated business. For this reason, instead of using pre–financing cash flows, the cash flows from all activities are used. These are the cash flows that will be available to equity holders and, since only cash flows to equity holders are considered, they need to be discounted by the cost of equity, rather than the cost of capital to the business (known as the weighted average cost of capital).

The free cash flow approach to valuation is depicted in *Figure 1.1* where the value of a business is the present value of the expected future free cash flows discounted at the appropriate cost of capital. To simplify the task of forecasting cash flows into perpetuity, typically cash flows are forecast over a finite time period, the planning period and any value beyond is captured in a terminal value.

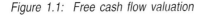
Figure 1.1: Free cash flow valuation

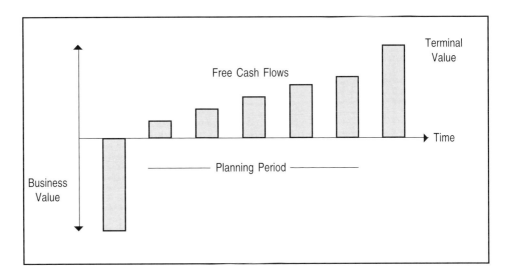

The critical issue to watch for is in terms of the interaction between the planning period and the terminal value. If the business is able to generate returns in excess of the cost of capital for a period of time, referred to as the competitive advantage period, which exceeds the planning period then the terminal value calculation will need to capture this ongoing value creation. These issues are considered more fully in *Chapters 4 and 5* and the mechanics of the free cash flow approach are reviewed in detail in *Chapter 3*.

2. Economic profit (EP)

Measures of economic profit focus upon the difference between the economic return on capital and the cost of capital invested in the company over a given time period. For example, if a company earns a 15% annual economic return on capital invested, its cost of capital is 10% and the capital invested is £1 million, then the economic profit generated is £50,000 ([15% – 10%] x £1m). Economic profit measures have been popularised through EVA® an approach trademarked by *Stern Stewart & Company*, and have an advantage over free cash flow approaches for purposes of measuring performance period by period.

Figure 1.2 depicts graphically a typical EP profile for a business which is able to generate positive EP's for its competitive advantage period. Typically, it is assumed that during the competitive advantage period competitors enter the market driving returns down to the cost of capital where no EP will be generated.

Figure 1.2: Economic Profit profile

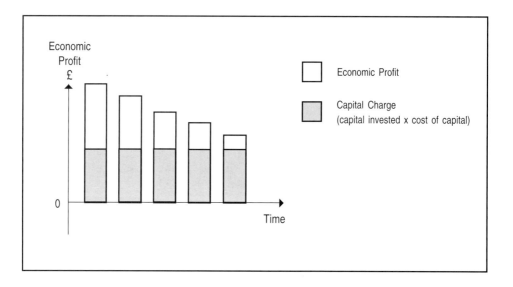

While economic profit focuses upon a given time period, Market Value Added (MVA), is used to show long–term total value creation or destruction. MVA represents invested capital plus the present value of projected economic profit figures. The one crucial difference between the two is that MVA embodies the markets expectations and it takes a forward–looking perspective. In fact, the results of applying free cash flow analysis and economic profit measures can be shown to be the same in principle when using the same assumptions [1]. *Figure 1.3* depicts the calculation of MVA at a point in time for a business.

Figure 1.3: Calculation of MVA

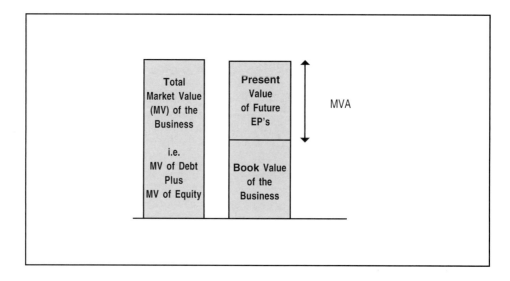

There are a number of variants of this economic profit approach, one being where equity cash flows are compared with the cost of equity to calculate an equity economic profit. For the reasons discussed earlier with reference to the free cash flow approach, this variant – would be that most likely to be adopted by a bank.

3. Cash Flow Return On Investment (CFROI)

CFROI attempts to measure the expected return on an investment, using its cash flows and considering the time value of money. In other words, it is a modified version of internal rate of return, designed for investments that have already been made. In the form in which it is used by its proponents, the CFROI for a firm is compared to the cost of capital to pass judgements on whether a company's investments are good, neutral or poor investments. To enhance its value then, a firm should increase the spread between its CFROI and its cost of capital.

This return on investment measure involves adjusting accounting returns and asset values to take account of inflation, asset lives, and depreciation. The real cash returns projected are compared to the company's inflation adjusted capital used to produce them.

Linking shareholder value and financial management

The implications of the drive to create shareholder value are profound. Companies that implement shareholder value typically adopt what has come to be known as Value Based Management (VBM) in some form that seeks to achieve the changes in behaviour and attitude consistent with creating value. VBM typically has important implications for all parts and functions of the business, not least of which is the finance function and financial management.

Good financial management is vital to the success of the business. Just as production management is concerned with handling physical resources at its disposal to increase corporate profitability and value, so financial management is concerned with improving the use of financial resources for the same objective. Financial resources represent the funds available to the business for which financial management is required to plan and control both their supply to and their use within, the business.

The traditional scope of financial management includes a number of key questions:

- Is the size and the composition of the present asset structure appropriate to the returns being achieved?

- What should be the size and composition of the future asset structure in relation to projected returns?

- What volume of funds is likely to be required to finance the future asset structure?

- What should be the composition of the capital structure both now and in the future?

A key issue in this book is the development of the link in principle between creating shareholder value and financial management. Against this, these key questions can be seen as follows:

Is the size and the composition of the present asset structure appropriate to the returns being achieved?

Figure 1.4: Hierarchy of ratios

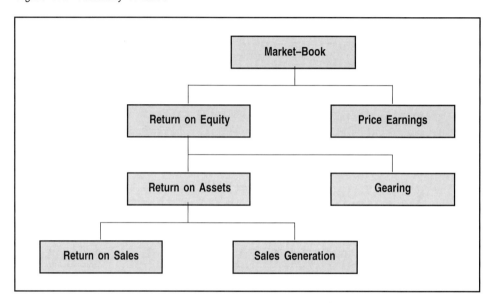

One of the most traditional approaches that can be use for interrogating the size and the composition of the capital base is the hierarchy (or pyramid) of ratios illustrated in *Figure 1.4*. At the top of this hierarchy is the market to book ratio that looks at the relationship between the market and book value of a business' equity. This can be broken down into the return on equity and the price earnings (PE) ratio, each of which can be further broken down. Accepting that any subset of ratios can be related to that in the level above, performance shortfalls can be assessed and analysed. For example, let us consider the following data:

- Profit   £5m

- Sales   £50m

- Fixed Assets   £30m

- Working Capital   £20m

In this case the return on assets is 10% (£5m ÷ (£30m + £20m), being the product of the return on sales is 10% (£5m ÷ £50) and the sales generation ratio is 1 (£50m ÷ £50m). If expectations had been for a return on assets of 15%, the return on sales ratio could be analysed to see whether costs had depressed the return, or the assets could be looked at in terms of the sales generated (sales generation ratio). Using this hierarchy attention can be directed to both the size and composition of the asset (and cost) base, however, that is not the end of the story. The criterion for creating value is the achievement of a return in excess of the cost of capital. The rationale for this being that nobody in his or her private life would invest in a business opportunity that yields a return less than the cost of funding it, so why accept this in business life. This being so, the return on assets should be benchmarked against the cost of funding them, as indicated in *Figure 1.5*.

Figure 1.5: Hierarchy of ratios and the cost of capital

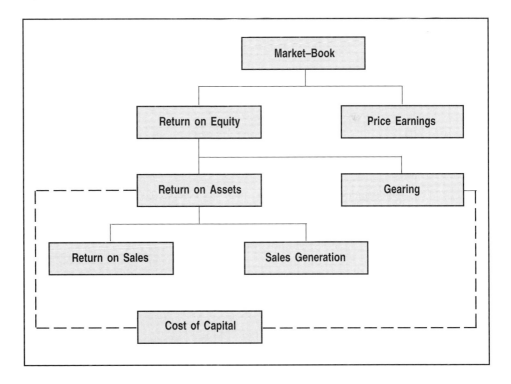

The difference between the return on assets and the cost of capital when multiplied by the capital invested gives a measure of the economic profit generated. This economic profit introduced earlier is a short–term measure of performance, but it can be converted to the long–term measure of value, MVA as discussed earlier and which will be reviewed in detail in *Chapter 6*.

What should be the size and composition of the future asset structure in relation to projected returns?

Concern within financial management is not only with the size and structure of the present asset structure, but also with future requirements. Such future requirements will typically be assessed in relation to prospective returns in relation to the perceived level of risk associated with the investment. This typically means looking at investments using project appraisal techniques and working capital in relation to its costs and benefits. However, what is relatively new is the move to link such decisions to the value of the business as a whole and shareholder value. As we will demonstrate, the value of a share and shareholder value is dependent upon perceptions of the future, which can be assessed by assessing prospective cash flows to be generated or the economic profit.

What volume of funds is likely to be required to finance the future asset structure?

Having projected the size and composition of the future asset structure for various parts of the business these need to be pulled together so that the cash flow implications in aggregate can be estimated. As will be illustrated in *Chapter 3*, the very process used for estimating the value of the based upon future projections can be used to assess the cash flow requirements and the likely volume of funds.

What should be the composition of the capital structure both now and in the future?

With a knowledge of the likely volume of funds the all important question can be asked, 'from what sources should capital be sought'. At its simplest this will be a decision about the relative proportion of debt and equity funding. The cost and implications of raising debt and equity differ and need to be taken into consideration. This issue will also be important in the valuation process because as will be shown in *Chapter 5*, different mixes of debt and equity result in different projected costs of capital, which in turn impact upon the business value.

Why focus on financial economics and shareholder value?

The rationale for the focus of attention can be thought of quite simply by drawing parallels with decisions of every day life. Nobody in his or her normal life would make a decision to invest for a return less than its cost. Therefore, one reason for focusing upon financial economics is to capture all costs, particularly those associated with funding debt and equity. This then raises the question about what return to compare this cost with. Given the tradition and development of accounting, could not the return be assessed with reference to accounting numbers. Sadly, as will be illustrated, the answer is no. Indeed, the rules of financial economics force attention to be directed towards cash flow, for one simple reason well captured in the following quote:

'Cash is fact, profit is opinion' [2]

Creative accounting

One particular problem with using profits or earnings for strategic analysis concerns creative accounting. This represents a means by which companies are able to create a favourable picture of their performance whilst doing nothing necessarily illegal [3]. Creative accounting featured strongly in the UK press, following the publication of a book by *Terry Smith* which was somewhat controversially entitled, *'Accounting for growth: how to strip the camouflage from company accounts'* [4]. *Smith* demonstrated a number of approaches by which companies could use and had used considerable judgement to produce results which put them in the best possible light, whilst staying within the letter of the law.

There are a number of well documented methods of creative accounting, but one potential creative accounting approach that can be used is to keep costs away from the profit and loss account by capitalising them. This is achieved by including them with fixed assets in the balance sheet. This is possible because accounting makes a distinction between costs that expire during an accounting period and are written–off through the profit and loss account, and assets, which do not expire during a single accounting period, and are 'held over'. If a case can be made for such items to be treated as assets, that part which expires during an accounting period will be matched as a cost, the remainder being held in the balance sheet as an asset.

Items that may often be capitalised include:

- Interest.

- Research and development.

- Start–up costs.

To understand how the capitalisation of costs works, consider the extreme case of a company which, after charging interest payable of £10 million through the profit and loss account, makes a loss of £5 million. Ignoring depreciation and any taxation issues, if this company did not include this interest payable in its profit and loss account, the loss of £5 million would be £5 million profit. This is because the £10 million of interest payable will be included with the fixed assets in the balance sheet rather than with costs in the profit and loss account. The books will still balance irrespective of the treatment of the interest payable and, in the case of the capitalisation of the interest, both the assets and the shareholders' fund sides of the balance sheet will have increased by £10 million [†].

When and why do companies capitalise interest costs? The practice may often be used, and not unreasonably, for a large project when the interest is considered to be an indistinguishable part of the cost of an asset. The effect of capitalisation is often very beneficial to the current year's profit but this may not be quite as much as just illustrated, because often the interest payable included within fixed assets will be depreciated together with the actual asset. For example, we will assume that our company with interest payable of £10 million incurs this in relation to a project with a planned time–scale of five years. Depreciating the project over five years means a reduction in profits for each year of £2 million, assuming a straight line write–off.

The effect of capitalisation is therefore to defer the cost, unless the item never makes an appearance in the profit and loss account – a practice that has been associated with the treatment of investment properties by companies in the property sector.

[†]   The shareholders' fund side of the balance sheet is higher because the loss of £5 million is now a profit of £5 million – a change of £10 million.

In principle, a skilled reader of company accounts should be able to spot creative accounting practices, however, there is some evidence that casts doubt on the ability of analysts to detect them [5]. For example, one piece of research found that of 1,325 possible corrections that the 63 experienced investment analysts could have made in calculating financial ratios from a set of accounts full of 'window dressing', only 34 adjustments were made in total. What is more, 52 analysts made no corrections at all! [6]

The international dimension

In addition to the potential problems of creative accounting there are some other difficulties in working with accounting–based measures that need to be brought into the discussion. These difficulties can be seen if we take a more international perspective. By way of illustration, *JBA Holdings*, a business applications software vendor, reported interim pre–tax losses as a result of having adopted US accounting standards. In fact, the result of restating 1996 results was the conversion of pre–tax profits of £1.4m to a loss of £2.42m [7]. Such situations are by no means new, and were well illustrated in 1993 when *Daimler–Benz* became the first German company to list its shares in New York. Under German rules, it reported a $372m profit; under tougher US ones, its loss was $1.1 billion! [8]

Such differences have also been well illustrated in studies of the European Union (EU) where, unlike many other parts of the world, a 'harmonisation' of accounting and financial reporting practices has been under way. However, the harmonisation of accountancy practices in the EU has been shown to have had limited impact, as was brought out many years ago in a study of seven EU states [9]. The preparers of accounts were asked to draft accounts (in ECU) for the same hypothetical group of companies to provide statements, which should be directly comparable as between different jurisdictions. For the profit and loss account, participants were asked to use the maximum flexibility of local rules to provide three alternative figures:

1. That at which a real company would be most likely to arrive,

2. The highest profit possible, and

3. The lowest profit possible.

The results of the study are summarised in *Table 1.1*.

Table 1.1: Profit differences within EU

	ECU millions		
	Most Likely Net Profit	**Maximum Net Profit**	**Minimum Net Profit**
Belgium	135	193	90
Germany	133	**140**	27
Spain	131	192	121
France	149	160	121
Italy	174	193	167
Netherlands	140	156	76
United Kingdom	192	194	**171**

The results of the study illustrated the potential for significant differences in reported net profits between EU member states. Also, that the range over which the profit may be measured could be different. To take extreme cases, the British profit could have been at worst 171m ECU while the German profit could have been at best 140m ECU. A major reason for the difference between the net profit figures concerned the treatment of goodwill. In an acquisition an acquiring company's financial reports include the target's assets and liabilities adjusted to fair value to reflect the total consideration paid. In the typical acquisition situation, where the amounts paid exceed the fair value of net assets acquired, the difference is classified as goodwill. Combined net income includes the target company's operating results only from the purchase date forward. Goodwill amortisation, adopted as standard practice in EU countries other than the UK, until recently, reduces such combined net income [†].

This study is now some eight years old and it is not unreasonable to believe that there has been greater progress towards harmonisation in financial reporting practices. In fact, more recent research has investigated the effect of the initiatives that have been undertaken by the International Accounting Standards Committee (IASC) which has been striving to put in place a set of core standards for acceptance by the world's leading stock markets [10].

[†] New mandatory rules imposed by the UK Accounting Standards Board (ASB) now require goodwill to be shown alongside a company's assets. Instead of writing–off goodwill immediately against reserves, companies will now be required to show goodwill as an asset and amortise it against future years profits. This will bring the UK in line with the practices adopted in most other countries.

In terms of general comparisons between EU financial reporting practices and the rest of the world, few differences were evident, probably because the EU contains the UK, France, and Spain, which are the ancestors for most of the accounting systems found internationally [11,12]. As regards the situation within EU countries, the results obtained suggested some important differences across the EU relating to specific issues (e.g. recognition of revenue on construction contracts, treatment of gains or losses on long–term monetary items, and the treatment of development costs).

The impression provided by the study is that the IASC has managed to reduce the number of options available to corporations, while at the same time permitting them to still employ the most commonly found practices. However, while the overall compliance rate with the IASC recommendations was found to be relatively high, considerable diversity still exists within the EU. What is more, harmonisation attempts by the EU appear to have had no influence on the extent to which EU practices are congruent with the IASC standards.

Until such time as standardisation is achieved it is appropriate to bear the following quote in mind:

> '...the sheer scale of international accounting differences including the effects of such complex figures as 'earnings' and 'net assets' means that income statement formats around the world are not only different, but also irreconcilable.' [13]

Value reporting

One plea often made is for the provision of more relevant information to those who use financial statements in making decisions about companies [14]. The view has been expressed that the financial reporting model is an anachronism that, despite increasingly tight regulation and extensive disclosure requirements, does not meet the needs of those who run businesses and invest in them [15]. To overcome this *PricewaterhouseCoopers* has proposed an approach called 'Value Reporting' which has seven core components [16].

1. Perform a preliminary evaluation of the financial drivers of the company – the levers of shareholder value.

2. Determine how these drivers are embodied in the corporation's objectives and how the drivers are shaping business operations.

3. Understand how management has developed the strategies currently in place to achieve these objectives.

4. Determine whether the objectives and strategies are supported by performance measurements, and assess the quality of measurement data provided to management.

5. Assess whether management processes foster value creation.

6. Draw up the 'big picture' from all of the foregoing activities and select the most relevant points to communicate with the investing public about value–creating strategies, processes, goals, and results.

7. Review, on a rotating basis, how effectively the major processes of the company (such as capital planning and acquisitions, budgeting, strategic planning, product/service planning, management forums, and executive compensation) are functioning, and fix what needs to be fixed.

Value reporting is characterised by a Statement of Shareholder Value Achieved, based on estimated future cash flows, which analyses financial and non–financial 'value drivers' over time. These are the key variables that lead to the creation of shareholder value. The examples of the kind of financial variables represented by these value drivers include:

- Sales growth rate.

- Profit margin.

- Cost of capital.

Non–financial drivers include:

- Market share.

- Customer satisfaction.

- Product defects.

- 'Intellect index', to gauge employees' skills, competencies and experience.

- Research and development.

- Brands.

- Indicators of administrative efficiency, such as process cost per sales transaction or office space utilisation.

This Statement of Value Achieved expresses the underlying value of the business as a whole and per share. How such value is calculated is reviewed in the next chapter.

Accounting measures and valuation

We have identified many limitations associated with accounting measures, which limit their value in strategic financial analysis. By and large, these have been discussed within the context of external reporting, but they have some additional limitations, when considered as internal measures of performance, i.e.

1. Risk is excluded.

2. Investment requirements are excluded.

3. Time value of money is ignored.

Risk is excluded

Risk is of central importance in establishing the economic value of any asset. A firm's level of risk is determined both by the nature of its operations and by the relative proportions of debt and equity used to finance its investments. These two types of risk are respectively referred to as 'business risk' and 'financial risk'. Earnings figures do not incorporate consideration of either type of risk.

Investment requirements are excluded

The relationship between changes in economic value and changes in earnings is further obscured by the fact that the investments in working capital and fixed capital needed to sustain the firm and to support future growth are excluded from the earnings calculation.

Time value of money is ignored

Earnings fail to measure changes in economic value because earnings calculations ignore the time value of money. Economic value calculations, by comparison, explicitly incorporate the idea that a sum of money received today is worth more than a sum of money received a year from now because it can be invested to earn a return over the next year. What is more, the discount rate used to estimate economic value can be adjusted to include not only compensation for risk-bearing, but also compensation for the expected levels of inflation.

The empirical evidence

Specific accounting based indicators of performance have been found in UK studies to fare poorly as measures of shareholder return, that is what shareholders expect to receive by way of dividends and capital appreciation. For example, studies have found that there is little if any statistical relationship between shareholder return and earnings per share growth and virtually no relationship at all with return on equity [17]. However, by comparison, cash flow measures fare much better than accounting measures of profitability as indicated by a considerable amount of empirical research, which has demonstrated that there is a significant relationship between cash flow and share prices [18]. Research undertaken in the UK supports previous work predominantly based upon United States data [19]. Using a sample of 98 firms listed on the London Stock Exchange over the period 1979 to 1992, strong evidence was found that cash flow variables have incremental information content beyond that contained in accrual earnings. However, both accrual earnings and cash flows were found to be important determinants of stock returns for UK companies.

As far as other markets are concerned, the evidence is far less comprehensive. In the Asia Pacific region, preliminary research has indicated that investors have not relied upon earnings per share growth to value securities, but are concerned with their overall potential cash payout, adjusted for risk [20].

There is little doubt that there have often been some consequences of adopting a shareholder value perspective in terms of employment, but what are the real consequences? Research by the *McKinsey Global Institute* has shown that a focus on shareholder value is second only to open and competitive product markets in accounting for high productivity [21]. A study of the relationship between shareholder value creation, labour productivity, and employment growth in competing countries across Germany, Japan and the United States found that winning companies are more productive, create more shareholder value, and grow employment faster than other players [22]. This research was broadened and deepened more recently in a study of the performance of more than 2,700 companies over a ten–year period [23]. Contrary to the view so often expressed by continental European companies, a focus on shareholder value was found to boost productivity and liberates resources to the benefit of all stakeholders in the long–term. A virtuous cycle was found linking shareholder value with overall economic performance. The way this cycle was found to operate at the country level was:

● A shareholder value focus at the country level expands employment opportunities because the distribution of the value created releases more disposable income in the economy.

● This in turn tends to produce more disposable income for consumption.

● This produces additional growth opportunities for companies, and;

● Generates more shareholder value.

Whilst shareholder value can be portrayed as the key part of the virtuous cycle, there is evidence as to the important contribution provided by customers, shareholders and employees, described in terms of 'corporate culture'. *Kotter and Heskett* compared 12 high– and 10 low–performing companies based on 11 years of financial performance from 1977 to 1988 [24]. High performers were compared with low performers from the same industries in order to make the results more meaningful. All were rated with respect to various aspects of their cultures, using survey data from industry analysts. The study found a strong link between adaptable, win/win, value–focused cultures and outstanding economic performance. Of particular note, is that the 12 financial high performers were rated significantly higher with respect to managing in the interests of customers, employees and shareholders. *Table 1.2* summarises the records of the 12 high performance firms versus the 10 low performers over the 11 years studied:

Table 1.2: *High versus low performance firms*

Performers	High	Low
Revenue growth	682%	166%
Work force growth	282%	36%
Share price increase	901%	74%
Net Income increase	756%	1%

The implications from such research are important to understand. Shareholder value may not be as alien to stakeholder interests as it is sometimes portrayed and stakeholders play a key role in the value creation process. This latter point has been recognised by the endeavours of those who motivate management using performance related pay. For example, *Danone* is cited as paying its managers bonuses of between 25% and 70% of their salaries that are based in part on economic value added [25]. Share options have also been introduced in Europe, but are more problematic, often being viewed by unions as being just means by which managers enrich themselves.

The new financial management and the new focus upon shareholder value in continental Europe

Much attention is being directed towards the issue of shareholder value within the context of continental Europe where, in many countries, there has been a tradition of greater concern with a broader stakeholder perspective. According to *Fortune*:

> 'The Euro isn't the only change rocking European business. Two decades after the US, the Old World's blue chips are finally getting the shareholder–value religion.' [26]

According to *Fortune*, the combined forces of deregulation, globalisation and the recession of the 1990s had demonstrated Europe's productivity shortcomings. With the liberalisation of financial markets, privatisations of $200bn, the demand for capital and the introduction of the Euro, CEOs in Europe are having to justify their strategies to the providers of funds, an increasing number of whom hail from the US. In fact, since 1990, the number of European companies listed on the New York Stock Exchange has quadrupled to 137, and many are very big players.

Nokia is quoted as a good example of one company that has adopted the shareholder value ethos after a long period of having previously put itself on the shelf. *Nokia's* refocusing did not come until it had suffered through huge losses, haemorrhaging sales, a capital famine, a management takeover, and exposure to the demands of Wall Street. Arguably, the same revolution will occur in other companies who will doubtless face the sort of crises *Nokia* suffered in the early 1990s.

Whilst the shareholder value movement in continental Europe gains momentum generally, there are some markets where the pace of change is noteworthy. Germany in particular has been identified as one important European market in which shareholder value is truly coming of age [27]. By all accounts, the *Deutsche Telekom* privatisation inspired a lively investor culture in a country where it had hardly existed before. Corporates are responding by pursuing strategies – in mergers and acquisitions, portfolio management, balance sheet restructuring, capital raising and investor relations – that focus on pleasing their shareholder base.

In fact, changes to German share buy back legislation last year were a major contributor to some of the value creating initiatives that have been adopted. After extensive lobbying by some of the larger companies, in May 1998 the government sanctioned the buy back by companies of up to 10% of their registered share capital over an 18 month period. There followed a six month period of uncertainty as regards the tax position of shareholders in such circumstances but, having resolved that, the pharmaceuticals group *Schering* undertook a buy back and *BASF* followed suit.

In such environments, the role of the CFO is going through a transformation. Traditionally the CFO was the conduit for control work and was heavily involved in treasury matters. Today, the CFO in Germany is more likely to be involved with the CEO in restructuring and planning, cost of capital analysis, investor relations, funding techniques and portfolio matters.

Changing role of finance

The finance function has an important part to play as an interface for top management decisions. Its overall involvement will include:

- Strategic planning, covering the development and monitoring of business plans (details and milestones), the establishment of the optimal capital structure and ensuring that the necessary funds are available to carry out the strategy;

- Managing the key financial relationships with outsiders: shareholders, the financial world, auditors, banks, the analysts, the authorities;

- The establishment and carrying out of financial policy: capital structure, dividend policy;

- Operational financial planning: capital expenditure programmes, cash planning, balance sheet planning;

- Treasury management, debt structure and gearing, the management of risk;

- Economic viability: performance measures and the budgeting system;

- Intragroup policies: reporting and bonus schemes;

- Quality control: information systems, standards, and procedures [28].

For successful businesses and particularly those embarking on a shareholder value initiative, there will be many important issues to address, but three that are crucial are:

- Strategy implementation: to ensure that the agreed strategy is proceeding according to plan. It is reckoned that financial managers have to keep the whole company under review, they have to ensure that the necessary control points are in existence, the milestones and responsibilities are mapped out and that everyone is aware of what they have to do.

- Strategic change: financial managers and their information systems have to respond to present day pressures.

- Strategic flexibility: finance has to be ready to respond fast to opportunities, which arise, e.g. new investment opportunities in Eastern Europe.

The ascendancy of the general financial manager

Financial management in some form or another is increasingly being seen as the responsibility of virtually every person in the firm [29]. For example, cost management is one such area and the importance being attached to it has significant implications for financial specialists like the management accountant [30]. There is a view that business pressures will impact upon the financial specialist such that the demand for management accountants as specialists may fall, while the need for management accounting more broadly may rise. Such an outcome would reflect a move towards decentralisation, which will mean greater general managerial responsibility for much of the traditional domain of the financial specialist. Taking this view, the management accountants who survive the transition will need to be highly skilled and:

- will become a part of their organisation's value–added team;

- participate in the formulation and implementation of strategy;

- translate strategic intent and capabilities into operational and managerial measures;

- move away from being score keepers of the past and to become the designers of the organisation's critical management information systems, besides being knowledgeable about cost management and management accounting! [31]

It seems that there will be pressure for some current responsibilities of the finance specialist to be driven down into the organisation, but there will also be a clearly defined role for central financial specialists. The responsibility for cost management will become increasingly the domain of all managers, but a breed of financial specialists will be required at the centre. The reason why the responsibility for cost management will become more general has been illustrated with reference to health service treatment protocols. These are standardised ways to treat a particular medical condition and are used in healthcare to reduce costs. The objective is to give physicians a concrete idea of the minimum cost procedure the average patient should receive to obtain effective treatment. The key point is that treatment protocols are developed and implemented by individuals with clinical knowledge, such that the management accountant becomes a key specialist with the responsibility for providing strategically critical information for managing costs [32].

The implications of these changes are that:

- As cost management becomes more important, so too does management accounting with the consequence that cost information currently not collected is required. This means that a firm's cost system often has to be upgraded. A key role of the management accountant will relate to the design of a system, but once designed the responsibility for its management will move to the workforce.

- Empowering the cost management process requires the decentralisation of the management accounting function.

- The management accounting function becomes one of supporting the broader workforce probably by way of being a member of a multi–skill team rather than as a member of a functional team of specialists, and also monitoring performance.

The overall implications are that finance and VBM will be the domain and responsibility of a broad based group of managers. While the financial specialists will be required to provide the guidance and direction, the implementation will be by general managers with business responsibilities that include financial management.

Summary checklist

- New metrics are being used to assess value creation and these include free cash flow analysis, economic profit and cash flow return on investment.

- The move to new metrics has been driven by the creative flexibility allowed by traditional accounting rules, the lack of harmonisation of international accounting standards and the limitations of accounting measures for valuation.

- Increasing evidence is being put forward to demonstrate that increasing shareholder value does not necessarily come at the expense of the organisations other stakeholders such as customers and employees.

- The role of finance is moving away from its historical role of financial control to a more pro–active and collaborative role as a strategic partner to the business.

- In adapting to its new role, finance will develop a number of its traditional activities to general managers within the business. As this happens finance will move to a more strategic role for decision making at the board level.

Chapter 2

Value Based Management

Chapter preview

- Value Based Management (VBM) as an approach for managing the value of a business.

- Critical questions that VBM must answer.

- Review of the experiences of organisation such as *Lloyds TSB* and *Hongkong and Shanghai Hotels* in implementing VBM.

- Scenario analysis as a powerful tool for gaining a strategic focus to VBM.

- Review of the four phases to implementing VBM together with associated issues.

What is Value Based Management?

Value Based Management (VBM) is an approach that can be used for the management of a business that differs from traditional approaches to managing a business insofar as it is linked with the principles of Discounted Cash Flow (DCF). As will be illustrated in the following chapters, DCF principles are typically used to develop a value–based strategy from which value based plans are developed and implemented as VBM.

The impetus to adopt VBM for managing the business is often associated with some external threat, like being a potential acquisition target. For example, *Ronnie Hempel*, the Chief Executive of *ICI* was reported as saying that the demerger into *ICI* and *Zenecca* was intended to allow *ICI* executives to concentrate on a narrower range of businesses, and to release what he referred to as 'creative management energies' [33]. By all accounts the company's focus upon profitability in the past was not as good as it should have been. A second illustration of the impetus to adopt VBM can be related to one of the most noteworthy adopters of the approach in the UK, *Lloyds TSB* a major retail bank. A major stimulus for focusing upon value came from poor past performance and prospects for the future if no corrective action was taken. For example, in the early 1980's before *Lloyds* embarked upon a shareholder value oriented approach, its shares were selling at less than book value: at the end of 1992 they were selling at 533p, or more than 240% of book value.

This ten year turnaround involved a number of steps which, when taken together, illustrated what can be achieved if the shareholder value concept is embraced. What *Lloyds* seemingly did was to:

● Rank its businesses on the basis of the shareholder value they had created. Each activity was viewed either as a creator or destroyer of value and businesses with a permanent negative cash flow became a target for divestment.

● Make provisions of about £3bn for problem country debt. This produced accounting losses but no movement in cash and as a result the share price went up, not down.

● Adopt higher value strategies such as expansion into life assurance and private banking which reduced the group's risk profile and increased its cash flow.

● Recognise that in measuring performance, 'cash is king'. Earnings per share and other accounting variables should not be used exclusively to assess performance, because they ignore the time value of money and exclude risk. This approach involved the inherent assumption that long term cash flows are what determines market value.

● Introduce performance related remuneration, thus linking the interest of its people more closely with those of the owners. Many employees now own shares in the company and senior management have serious money at stake in shareholdings in the company and/or shareholder options.

The *Lloyds TSB* experience indicates that attention to shareholder value gave it clear discipline. The company's goal has been to analyse every strategic decision in terms of its impact on shareholder wealth. It also focuses upon shareholder value to evaluate acquisitions, divestments, capital investment projects, and to assess alternative strategies. *Lloyds TSB* recognises that it now has the tools to manage its companies better from a strategic and financial standpoint. Furthermore it has made some serious attempts in implementing the approach, but it also does recognise that it has a long way to go. Nevertheless, *Lloyds TSB* has taken the approach very seriously and sees it as having an important part to play in the bank's future.

Company involvement with VBM can be seen in terms of those that:

1. Have adopted various value analytical techniques but not yet the broader managerial implications of the approach.

2. Have embraced the underlying principles of a value–based approach and have also embarked upon implementation.

3. Do not appear to have experimented at all.

4. Claim to be value oriented companies but whose actions do not support this impression.

There appear to be many companies which fall into 1 above and which do not appear to have experimented at all. There also seem to be many companies espousing the pursuit of maximising shareholder value in their annual reports but whose apparent interpretation of this would appear to be focused towards accounting based measures like earnings per share. A number of companies fall into the third category, but all indications point to relatively few that have embarked on any broad based implementation.

Companies recognised as having moved substantially towards full–scale implementation include a number of US companies like *Coca–Cola, AT&T, Quaker Oats, Briggs & Stratton*, and *CSX*. For example, *AT&T's* decision in 1993 to buy *McCaw Cellular* for $12.6bn was reported as having been influenced significantly by valuation principles [8]. In the UK, a systems solutions business, *ICL* is a good example of a company that has expended considerable effort in implementing a value based approach for managing the business via its business value programme.

VBM implementation steps

Assuming the decision to proceed with implementing VBM has been taken and that there is strong corporate sponsorship for the process, the steps that need to be taken can be summarised as determining:

1. What is the managerial interpretation of your current value in the market?

2. What is influencing it, i.e. what are the key value drivers?

3. What are the apparent managerial actions for improvement and what is their impact?

Addressing these questions will give rise to a subset of important questions, like:

● What is the Competitive Advantage Period (CAP)? How do you know?

● What is the cost of capital?

● How should the terminal value be estimated?

● Which measures of value should be used?

● What frameworks should be used to guide managerial and employee actions?

The benefit of adopting a VBM perspective is best understood with reference to an example and in what follows we will draw upon the circumstances surrounding an Asian hotel group to illustrate many of its features. There is good reason for this choice. Every reader should be familiar with the kind of business and the circumstances of the Asian crisis, which exemplifies well some of the problems associated with measuring value.

Hongkong and Shanghai Hotels Limited

Company Background

One of the best know sights on the Hongkong skyline is the Peninsula Hotel, a key part of the portfolio of the *Hongkong and Shanghai Hotels Limited*. In fact, the company was founded as *The Hongkong Hotel Company Limited* in 1866, more than 60 years prior to the opening of the Peninsula Hotel. The change of name to include Shanghai occurred in 1917 following the acquisition of the *Shanghai Hotels Limited*.

The *Hongkong and Shanghai Hotels Limited*, (the "Company" or "HK&S") is a listed company, but is closely held by its Directors and seven (7) major shareholders who hold approximately 50% of outstanding shares. Initially limited to properties in Hongkong, it diversified and embarked on an oversees expansion program, and now has interests in projects in the United States, Australia, Indonesia, Thailand, the People's Republic of China, the Philippines and Vietnam. Its principal business comprises the ownership and management of prestigious hotel, commercial and residential properties in key destinations in Asia, Australia and the US; its hotel management arm is The Peninsula Group. Group investments are summarised in *Figure 2.1*:

Figure 2.1: Listing of investments by geographic location

Hongkong	The Peninsula
	The Kowloon Hotel
	The Repulse Bay Complex
	St. John's Building
	The Peak Tower
	The Peak Experience
	Tai Pan Laundry
	Peninsula Clubs and Consultancy Services
Australia	Bennelong, Sydney
Indonesia	Kota Ciputra, Jakarta
Thailand	The Peninsula Bangkok
Mainland China	The Palace Hotel, Beijing
The Philippines	The Peninsula Manila
United States of	The Peninsula New York
America	The Sutton, New York
	The Peninsula Beverley Hills
	Quail Lodge, Carmel Valley
Vietnam	The Landmark, Ho Chi Minh City
	Giang Vo, Hanoi

The currency crisis in the latter half of 1997 had a major impact upon The Company, with the company's share price falling to HK$5.50 at the end of 1998.

Table 2.1 provides a summary of the company's reported financial data.

Table 2.1: *Hongkong and Shanghai Hotels – Summary of reported financial data*

Balance Sheet as at December	1998	1997	1996	1995	1994
HK$ millions					
Net Assets	16,981	24,108	25,887	20,262	19,629
Shareholders' Equity	10,267	18,166	21,671	16,416	16,053
Ordinary Shares	578	581	586	539	539
Revaluation Reserves	8,210	14,211	16,762	13,189	13,155
Net Debt	6,689	5,406	3,873	3,597	3,398
Other data	**1998**	**1997**	**1996**	**1995**	**1994**
HK$ millions					
Sales	2,140	2,779	2,674	2,318	1,785
Share Price at period end [HK$]	5.50	6.40	14.6	11.2	8.95
Market Capitalisation at BS date	6,364	7,441	17,100	12,084	9,657
Number of Shares at BS date (millions)	1,157	1,163	1,171	1,079	1,079

The VBM approach

To illustrate the VBM approach for *HK&S* and to introduce the substance of subsequent chapters, we will draw on the following three questions that were introduced earlier:

1. What is the managerial interpretation of your current value in the market?

2. What is influencing it, i.e. what are the key value drivers?

3. What are the apparent managerial actions for improvement and what are their impacts?

What is the managerial interpretation of your current value in the market?

The share price at the end of 1998 was HK$5.50m making the market value of the equity HK$6,364 million. At the same time the value of net debt was HK$6,689 million. This is for a business whose net assets stood at the last full balance sheet date as HK$16,981 million. The implications of this are that the business is a value destroyer. Net assets of HK$16,981 million look from a market perspective as though they are to be used to create a value of HK$13,053 million (HK$6,364 million plus HK$6,689 million). As such, this business could be seen as a potential acquisition target if it was not closely held.

In later chapters, we will consider how this business value and the share price might be interpreted from a managerial perspective.

What is influencing it, i.e. what are the key value drivers?

As will be demonstrated in *Chapter 6* the starting point we recommend is to understand the current share price of HK$5.50 in terms of the key factors that drive it. These factors are known as 'value drivers' and, in our experience, they are important to understand because all too often businesses do not really know what is driving value. This can be for a number of reasons, not least of which is that the key factors may have changed. For example, a management college set up in the 1940s designed to provide non–qualification experiential training to potential board members might have a prime countryside location as a key value driver for attracting potential customers. Fifty years on when the bulk of the income is driven from a distance learning graduate MBA programme for which students do not attend, location may not be such a key value driver. In the minds of such students and to the market if it was a publicly traded business, other factors, like the quality of communications, are likely to be far more important. There might still be those living in the past who believe location to be important, but the problem is that their perception of the allocation of resources into maintaining the quality of the premises in the UK as distinct from other choices, might actually destroy value. Alternatively, if the value drivers have not changed it may be the case that the relationship between changes in their value and the impact upon share price is not known. For example, in one acquisition in which we were involved it was evident that the potential acquirer would raise margins in the target business. While it was appreciated that such action would increase the share price, the extent of the increase was not appreciated until a simple financial model had been built.

What are the apparent managerial actions for improvement and what are their impact?

Having valued the business and identified the key value drivers, the next critical step is to understand how to translate them into measures of performance that are understood and can be implemented such that there is the incentive to take the necessary action.

The strategic perspective and scenario analysis

Our experience has shown that this VBM approach has also to be viewed from a strategic perspective. Much more will be said about strategic issues in *Chapter 4*. For now, we provide an overview of strategic thinking that we use as a reality check against action for the future that might be proposed [34]. For example, the share price of HK$5.50 per share for *Hongkong and Shanghai Hotels Limited* might be shown to increase drastically as a consequence of completely refocusing of the business outside Asia. In the absence of testing this against the potential consequences of such a move it is pure speculation. That is where scenario thinking becomes particularly important and as a consequence of such analysis a number of critical issues can be addressed, that include:

1. What are the business' prospects according to your scenarios?

2. What is driving the prospects?

3. What is the value of these prospects?

4. Do these prospects make sense?

5. What should be the business response?

Scenario analysis

Scenarios start from the premise that there is more than one future and recognise the need to illuminate the major forces and trends driving a valuation, their interrelationships, and the critical uncertainties. Scenarios need not be heavily driven by mathematical or statistical analysis. *Shell*, for example, when applying this technique does not assign probabilities to its scenarios for several reasons. First, it intentionally looks at several scenarios that are more or less equally plausible, so that none is dismissed out of hand. Second, by definition, any given scenario has only an infinitesimal probability of being right because so many variations are possible. Third, the reason to be hesitant about all scenario quantification is that there is a very strong tendency for people to clutch at the numbers and ignore the more important conceptual or structural messages [35]. The value of performing this procedure is not so much the ultimate valuation number that it produces, but the insights discovered in the process of investigating the nature and existence of the opportunities available to management.

Specifically, the use of scenarios can help to avoid the shortcomings associated with traditional approaches to analysis, in which the assumptions used will often be extrapolated from the present situation with inadequate attention being paid to the impact of changes in the external environment of a particular business. With these traditional approaches, instead of a specific impact analysis there is an assumed vacuum, as if discontinuation and turbulence will not punctuate the external environment. Drawing upon scenario analysis can make considerable improvements. When linked appropriately, to free cash flow and strategic value calculations, it provides a distinctive way of grasping the key navigational questions about the future of a business. In terms of the CAP, the approach seeks to force questioning and thought about when the conditions signalling the end of the CAP might occur, i.e. a return greater than the cost of capital cannot be achieved. This involves asking key questions like – 'How can the free cash flow projections be validated for that period?' and ' Suppose the business under consideration is moving into a period of increasing turbulence?' To cope with that, it may become a significantly different business, or it may fail to cope and as a result under–perform relative to its original plan, which assumed little turbulence.

It is usually easy to imagine at least two different free cash flow projections, and the benefit from going through more than one projection and discovering the linkages typically enhances managers' learning, not least because many predictions are often mistaken. Scenarios help to avoid mistakes and can be seen in quite simple terms as being long term 'stories' about possible future external environments, framed as two or three credible pathways.

Scenarios oblige the recognition of the dependencies that business performance has on external factors over which a firm has no control (like rain), but to which it might be able to respond in a timely manner (like an umbrella available before the next rainfall). They also encourage thinking through a welter of diverse speculations and the structuring of these into coherent pathways, which are relevant to a particular business. The pay–off is that, in terms of the scenarios, the impact on the business of such external factors can be estimated. This enables an analysis of the potential value of the business to be undertaken, not with one straight–line calculation, but with different higher and lower values.

The risk of unwittingly making the analysis of strategic value abstract occurs when it is detached from the real business environment. This can occur when the assumptions underlying the numbers in a business plan, when put through the strategic value model, are not challenged but implicitly treated as a matter of faith. The risk is that of being mesmerised by numerical calculations whilst overlooking the possibility that the plan itself assumes a single–track extension of the current business into the future CAP.

By contrast, the link between strategy and scenarios forces attention on a wide–ranging search for developments in the external environment, favourable or not, which can help managers to anticipate and adjust for the potential impact on the value drivers of changes in the environment. It means surfacing and challenging the assumptions behind the numbers given for the value drivers. Developing scenarios does not mean mechanically changing business variables by a fixed percentage. Instead, it means developing a comprehensive set of assumptions about how possible futures may evolve and how they are likely to affect industry profitability and the company's performance.

Scenarios start from 'What if...?' questions. By depicting future pathways which are different from the pathway assumed in a particular plan, adopted or proposed, the uncertainties about the plan can be highlighted. As scenarios express in a patterned way uncertainties about what external factors could impact on the value drivers, there should be at least two scenarios, preferably equally credible, to be posed against each other. Comparison of their respective impact on one or more value drivers would clarify the issues or challenges distinctive to each scenario which managers could confront in the future. Those issues would surface by grasping the impacts of each scenario on value drivers such as sales growth rate, operating profit margin and fixed and working capital requirements, and the cost of capital. Thus the working out of different potential values for a business, based on scenarios, gives more flexibility, realistic relevance and 'navigational' value to the analysis of strategic value.

By means of scenarios the variables which could impact on a business's long term value may be identified. For example, for a manufacturing business which has outperformed rivals in the past, credible ideas as to what trends would constitute one scenario which includes increasing customer power, loss of differentiation, more intense cost/price competition, falling margins can be identified. All of these arise from a mix of factors, which range from the growth of international competition to the growing added–value ability of distributors.

Focusing on say the first five years of the example at hand, the impact on the five cash flow drivers of external conditions beyond the immediate control of the company may be illustrated by means of different credible scenarios. Armed with scenario outcomes the firm can mentally and practically prepare to see the earliest signs of change in its external environment. In effect it can, on a hypothetical basis, perceive in advance that if its key strategic challenges were to unfold – very differently from the alternative – what responses would be required. In other words, management can anticipate – initially on a 'What if?' basis – that to achieve, say, the sales receipts in the original plan, product and process technology changes would be required by a steep escalation in fixed and working capital investment needs.

Scenarios express and structure uncertainties about the future: of themselves they cannot resolve this uncertainty. But sharp and sensitive mental preparation by advance calculation of the value impact of alternative scenarios enables faster responses to be made. In this case, improved thinking about the substantive issues – the business challenges – raised by each scenario could lead to a planning process that enables an anticipated challenge, indeed a threat, to be converted by virtue of well–timed and scaled company response into an opportunity.

The materials chosen for scenarios may be brief and prosaic, formulated without recourse to larger–scale constructions about economic, political and other macro changes. But they are sufficient to illustrate the point that current assumptions used for estimating the future value of a business must be specified in credible speculations about the future and structured in such ways as to show how different future conditions can impact on the key value drivers.

The process of working out present value and CAP implications of different scenarios enables managers to make two important gains in their strategic thinking:

- They can see how the strategic value outputs derived from the inputs of their preferred or current plans depend on assumptions, which could be clarified and critically evaluated by comparisons made with the assumptions of credible alternative scenarios. Managers would therefore focus on the quality of their assumptions, about changes in the external environment, as a precondition of any confidence in the numbers subsequently generated through the Strategic Value Analysis model.

- Wrestling with each scenario's present value and CAP implications should sharpen managers' sense of the range of options they could have in driving forward their business in one direction or another. It gives a mental grip on how to weigh up in advance the risk/gain possibilities under each scenario.

There is however a third benefit. Each scenario helps to clarify the dominant strategic challenges associated with it – and how different (or similar) would the responses to each challenge have to be. Here is where the real and rapid advance in strategic thinking can occur. Consequences revealed through free cash flow analysis and strategic valuation help to clarify the first candidates for an effective strategic response. For example, these could be how an initial reactive response towards a threat might be converted into an opportunity, or how an attempt to respond to two different scenarios instead of wagering on one against another might yield a strategy aimed at resiliency against more than one possible future.

In our experience it is rare for the outcome of the application of scenario analysis to produce a CAP corresponding with the stretched market implied duration CAP which is explained in *Chapter 4*. The consequence of this is that the terminal value issue, so neatly dealt with by virtue of the definition of market implied duration, raises its head again. Typically, the CAP resulting from scenario analysis is considerably shorter than that for the stretched version. This means that the all important question of terminal value arises. In very simple terms, the terminal value implied is the difference between the market–implied price and the value of the scenario. Analysis of the terminal value arising from this difference can be undertaken to see the assumptions implied. For example, a significant difference between the perpetuity value of the terminal value determined from scenario based calculations and the market implied terminal value can be examined in terms of the implications by way of prospective growth assumptions. This examination can be by way of an extension of the scenario activity, in which external financial observations are challenged in terms of their managerial implications for the value drivers within the strategic value model. In other words, 'What rate of growth is implied by the difference and what would be necessary to make it happen?'

Key issues to consider in implementing VBM

There are some key phases that are essential in implementing VBM, which are the:

1. Introduction of concepts and gaining of corporate commitment.

2. Establishment of policies and procedures.

3. Integration of concepts into practice.

4. Development and refinement of the approach.

Phase 1

The introduction of concepts and the gaining of commitment can take some time. We would expect it to take a minimum of six months. It will involve:

● Presentations to senior corporate and divisional management of the concepts and its potential benefits to the company.

● Discussing key concerns and issues, e.g. value based executive compensation.

● Obtaining commitment of the managing director and key corporate and divisional management.

Phase 2

Establishing policies and procedures will often require considerable time and effort. In our experience, quite how much time is often dependent upon the size of the organisation, but as a rough guide six months is manageable if ambitious. More specifically, this phase will involve the:

● Formation of a 'task force', e.g. drawn from senior central management and divisions.

● Identification of specific obstacles and issues, e.g. how to relate the approach to the corporate financial management and reporting culture.

● Determination of appropriate divisional costs of capital, terminal value frameworks, and planning periods.

● Development of appropriate applications at corporate and divisional level.

● Development of application guidelines.

● Identification of education requirements of those employees who will perform or need to understand the approach.

● Development of education programmes.

Phase 3

The integration of concepts into practice, is the longest and probably the most critical part of the implementation process. Nine months is a rough and ready guideline, the actual length of time is heavily linked to the size of the organisation and how extensively the approach is to be introduced. In particular it typically involves the development of a framework that makes explicit recognition of the need to ensure a strong customer focus. Whilst the first two phases are important, the reality is that without explicit attempts to integrate principles with practice, the only deliverable will be a valuation shell. Achieving a strong customer focus may sound straightforward in principle, but the practice is more difficult. The aspiration to be customer oriented may be easily thwarted without recognition that it may have broader organisational ramifications. It is one thing to have the aspirations to be customer focused, but it is quite another to be able to meet such requirements. This will be particularly so in turbulent market conditions in which the areas in which internal excellence is required to achieve customer satisfaction may be difficult to say the least. The ways in which such customer orientation will be attempted differ, but approaches we will review in *Chapter 7* are the balanced scorecard and the business excellence model. Once these issues have been considered carefully, other initiatives that need to be undertaken include:

- Incorporation of the approach into performance measurement via financial and non–financial performance measures.

- Delivery of education programmes on the approach and how it links to current practices.

- Use of the approach for evaluating capital expenditure plans, acquisitions, research and development expenditure, and so on.

- Provision of expert assistance when needed.

Phase 4

The last phase, is very much an open book as regards the time involved. What it is likely to involve is the:

- Refinement of the approach and performance measurement.

- Linking of the approach to incentive compensation schemes.

- Development of the approach for investor communications.

The phases and underlying activities outlined above are by no means definitive but they a typically consistent from organisation to organisation. However, there will need to be some tailoring to particular circumstances of each organisation. So, whilst the basic building blocks of VBM are fairly consistent the exact recipe varies.

Summary checklist

- Using the principles underlying discounted cash flow, businesses have been adopting Value Based Management in order to manage the value of their business.

- Several companies have already started on the value journey which involves a number of steps, like – estimating the value of the business, identifying the key factors driving that value, identifying the value of the business in terms of performance measurement and management, and demonstrating how management and employees can be motivated and guided to respond in a way that will create value.

- Scenario analysis is a powerful strategic analysis tool for resolving some of the questions raised above in that it acts as a reality check for some of the actions for the future that might be proposed.

- Implementation of VBM involves a number of phases comprising different activities. The exact nature of these phases and activities will vary and have to be tailored to each individual organisation.

Chapter 3

Valuing the Business

Chapter preview

- The importance of assessing strategic value.

- The principles that underpin the free cash flow estimation of strategic value, drawing particularly upon information relating to an example company.

- How to calculate the strategic value of a business using a free cash flow value driver framework.

- The relationship between the value drivers, life cycle effects and the type of business being valued.

- The relationship between business value, corporate value and strategic value.

- A review of sources of information available to estimate strategic value.

Business valuation in context

This chapter is concerned with how future free cash flows and the value from a strategic investment opportunity (strategic value) can be estimated. The reason for its estimation is that there has to be a benchmark from which managerial action can be directed. In our experience we have found that being able to explain the value of the business in terms of how the market currently sees it is the most appropriate approach. Once a valuation model has been built and its implications understood, the key value drivers of the business should be apparent. Such value drivers, that represent the levers that have the greatest impact upon business value, provide the best reference point from which to direct future managerial action. This is notwithstanding the need to ensure that the strategic direction of the business has been appropriately challenged.

As will be illustrated, strategic value can represented by two related parts, that from the period over which forecast plans are made, known as planning period, and the period beyond, known as the continuing period. Associated with each of these will be a value, the size of which will depend upon a number of factors, including the type of business to be analysed.

The starting point on the journey to estimate strategic value is the estimation of the free cash flows using five value drivers, i.e.

1. Sales growth rate.

2. EBITDA (Earnings Before Interest Tax Depreciation and Amortisation) margin.

3. Cash tax rate.

4. Fixed capital investment.

5. Working capital investment.

Once these five have been reviewed, two more will be introduced in the form of:

6. The planning period.

7. The cost of capital.

Using these seven value drivers an illustration of how a picture of value can be estimated will be provided.

Estimating free cash flow

Given the focus of attention upon VBM and the quest to understand how to create value from better management, let us assume a business that has a five–year strategic plan, which it wishes to evaluate. As will be illustrated, this five–year plan can be valued from these five cash flow value drivers. The all important question is, how can values for the free cash flow drivers be estimated? The answer is that they are typically estimated by looking at a mix of past experience, management judgement about what is likely to happen in the future, and observations about the marketplace.

The importance of cash flow data should not be underestimated in measuring strategic value. The expression Garbage In, Garbage Out (GIGO) is very appropriate for issues relating to business valuation, where the quality of any business valuation can only be as good as the input data upon which it is based. With this in mind let us review the issues associated with estimating the cash flow drivers.

Sales growth forecasts

Estimated future sales can be projected from market information to produce forecasts about the market for goods or services. Such market forecasts should be based upon an analysis of market opportunities. A pricing policy will also have to be established in each sector in order to put a monetary value on the forecast sales quantities. Prices (in most markets) affect the quantity sold, so there will be an iterative process to estimate the sales volume at the most appropriate prices to provide what is thought to be the relevant sales receipts over the forecast period.

The current level of sales (for each product at current prices) is very much the starting point for sales growth analysis. Any expected growth in sales volume from, for example, prior investment in fixed and working capital must be added. There may also be some adverse influences upon sales value, for example, as a result of a decrease in sales volume because of say divestment, or even a lowering of prices.

As a starting point it can be quite helpful to think of the first driver of business value as being sales growth. If the enterprise does not sell anything, then it cannot really be said to be in business! However, it is important to be realistic in assessing sales growth potential. Current and prospective competition, when combined with actual and potential barriers to entry typically influence sales growth potential.

EBITDA margin

EBITDA is used rather than other measures of earnings, such as operating profit to overcome many of the difficulties that may arise because of taxation and capital structure differences, particularly within a cross–border valuation context [†]. It can also be thought of as being closer to cash than other measures of profit, because the depreciation of tangible assets and the amortisation of intangible assets are ignored in its calculation [‡].

EBITDA reflects the earnings to be generated after the costs of doing business have been taken into consideration. Typically, once sales forecasts and more concrete sales plans are agreed, managers will need to consider the means of ensuring the supply of those sales to customers, and the costs of doing so. Such costs will relate to:

1. the sourcing and costs of raw materials;

2. employing and training an adequate labour force;

3. establishing sufficient sales and distribution facilities;

4. marketing of the product/service;

5. ensuring adequate production facilities;

6. creating a management team able to manage the business.

[†] In circumstances, EBITDA information may not be available in which case the operating profit will typically need to be converted to cash flow by adding back depreciation and any other non–cash items.

[‡] Depreciation can be thought of as being an apportionment of the sum paid for a fixed asset over its useful economic life. The simplest way to understand this is with reference to an illustration. Imagine a piece of machinery bought today for £100,000, which is expected to last for 5 years, and to be worth nothing at the end of this time period. If paid for by cash then there would be a cash outflow of £100,000 at the time of purchase. However, for accounting purposes it would be written–off over the 5–year period, such that only a proportion, say one fifth or £20,000, would be charged against profit each year.

In a not–for–profit organisation, activities will also generate costs that have to be charged against income receivable. However, in some not–for–profit concerns, the income may not be linked to the service in quite the same way that costs are linked to sales in a commercial enterprise. For example, a charity in which the income from donations and grants is unrelated to the 'output' or activity of the charity. In this case, the not–for–profit undertaking has to ensure that the best use is made of its income by providing a cost–effective service. It is arguably more difficult to manage this – where one is measuring benefits against costs – than in the commercial world where the amount of profit is a measure of the degree of success.

What this illustration also flags up is that very different approaches may need to be adopted in generating forecast cash flows depending upon circumstances. What drives cash flow is by no means common to all types of business operations. A sequence of events starting with sales growth may be difficult to apply in all circumstances.

It is important to realise that the EBITDA margin on sales also depends on the type of business. Generally, the principle is that the greater the need for investment in fixed assets and working capital, the higher the profit margin has to be on sales. For example, food retailers in the UK have relatively low amounts tied up in fixed assets and working capital. They may own some of their stores, but also rent others, and have very little tied up in working capital by way of stocks and debtors. Such companies work on lower sales margins than heavy goods companies, like those supplying plant and equipment to industry, that have to plan for much higher margins on sales value. Such companies have large factories to pay for and the net profit on each sale has proportionately to be much higher than the retailer.

Cash tax flows

Once EBITDA has been estimated, a forecast amount of tax to be paid will have to be taken into account. Tax is often more difficult to consider from a general managerial perspective than the other cash flow drivers because it is very much a specialist area. For this reason, general assumptions about the cash tax rate are often made when valuing a business, nevertheless, there are one or two issues that are important for you to understand.

First, tax payable upon profits is an income tax paid by a venture on its income (or net profit) in just the same way that individuals have to pay income tax on their income. Companies in many countries must also pay capital gains tax on any gain made from liquidating an asset or investment held over time. For example, if an office building were sold for £10m which had originally cost £4m, there would be tax to pay on the capital appreciation of £6m. However, in many countries the capital gains tax is not levied on the full capital gain because an allowance is made for the general rate of inflation. In this example, the allowance for inflation would mean that the £4m original cost would be indexed to a higher figure and the resultant gain would be lower.

Secondly, a charge, for what has become known as deferred tax, is made in each year's accounts for a number of adjustments, including the amount of capital gains tax that would have to be paid if the asset were sold at the date the accounts were drawn up. The main point about deferred tax is that it is irrelevant as far as free cash flow is concerned. The concern is with the amount of tax actually paid in any year, that is the year during which any tax is payable.

Thirdly, under taxation systems like that in the UK, interest payable is a tax–deductible expense, whereas as a general rule, interest receivable and investment income are taxable income. In other words, for a company with a net interest expense, the tax charge in the profit and loss account has been reduced by the tax shield effect of interest. To arrive at the true after–tax profits from operations, the tax charge must first be adjusted to reverse this effect. This can be estimated by multiplying the net interest payable figure in the profit and loss account by the marginal rate of corporation tax. The adjusted tax charge effectively represents the tax payable by the company if it had been entirely equity–financed, and had no non–operating income. If this adjustment is not made, the way in which a company has been financed will distort the calculated return.

Fixed and working capital investment

Using information about sales growth potential, the EBITDA margin and likely cash tax payments, operating cash flows can be estimated. However, for valuation purposes free cash flow estimates are required in the form of deductions from operating cash flow for investment purposes. In other words, the distinction between operating cash flow and free cash flow is that investment necessary to maintain existing cash flows and to support future cash flows both of which need to be taken into consideration in deriving free cash flow. Such investment will be concerned with:

- Fixed capital investment in the form of investment for the replacement of fixed assets to meet existing customer demands (RFCI) and investment in new assets to meet intended sales growth projections (IFCI).

- Working Capital Investment (WCI), that is investment in working capital, such as stocks of materials.

Estimating these can be difficult in practice, and many different approaches can be adopted. For RFCI, the objective is to assess how much a company needs to reinvest in its existing core business, at current prices, in order to maintain both the productive capacity and where it is an issue, competitive position. In other words, how much should the company be charging against profits for the use of its fixed assets on a replacement cost basis? This number is often referred to as the 'maintenance capex (capital expenditure)' and its calculation forces an assessment of the real economic value of a company's assets. Companies tend to invest according to their free cash flow and so an analysis of free cash flow should give a reasonable guide to a company's future investment spending. This is because falling free cash flow is often followed by falling capital investment and vice–versa. Since companies are not obliged to disclose the

RFCI, any assessment of its value is bound to be subjective. However, in some industries, maintenance capex can be estimated with some degree of confidence by referring to the replacement cost of capacity e.g. airlines, car manufacturers and steel producers. In other industries, however, the figure may bear little relationship to the eventual cost of replacing fixed assets. More generally, an estimate of maintenance capex must be put in the context of both actual capex and historic cost accounting (HCA) depreciation figure. Actual capex over several years, relative to sales or fixed assets, gives a guide to how much a company has thought it necessary to invest in its assets – though this must be offset by an assessment of the proportion of that capex that was earmarked for expansion rather than maintenance. HCA depreciation in most cases provides a baseline figure for maintenance capex, such that a frequently used assumption is that depreciation is a good estimate for RFCI.

For the other two types of investment, IFCI and WCI, there are many different forecasting approaches. One approach mentioned above, which will be illustrated in the next section, involves estimating the relationship between increased sales and increased fixed and working capital expenditure using historical data. It is important to note that this will very often need to be disaggregated substantially. For example, working capital investment will typically be analysed in terms of required expenditure on individual components, like stocks and debtors.

Perhaps the most difficult problem in this area arises when there are step changes in technology. If a competitor invents a new production process, which dramatically lowers cash operating costs, a company is obliged to decide whether to invest in the same technology or face a steady loss of competitive position. Even if it judges that the return on that investment will be inadequate, once a rival's capacity is in existence it will tend to drive industry prices down to new, lower, levels relative to input costs. In effect, this means that a decision not to invest is a decision to begin to leave the industry.

Whilst reference has been made to fixed and working capital requirements to support future growth, they are not the only type of investment that may be necessary. Expenditure on research and development, product development as well as other less tangible items, may be required. The reality is that this is a cash flow approach which recognises that any cash outflow, however defined for accounting purposes, must be taken into consideration.

Illustration – estimating free cash flow

To see how the five cash flow value drivers can be used to provide a free cash flow estimate, let us consider a hypothetical company called *Omega plc* with sales revenue today of £300m and the value driver profile illustrated in *Table 3.1*:

Table 3.1: Value driver profile

Year	1	2	3	4	5	Beyond
	%	%	%	%	%	%
Sales Growth Rate (SGR)	5	5	5	5	5	0
EBITDA Margin	10	10	10	10	10	10
Cash Tax Rate (CTR)	30	30	30	30	30	30
IFCI	10	10	10	10	10	0
IWCI	10	10	10	10	10	0
Cost of Capital	10	10	10	10	10	10
	£m	£m	£m	£m	£m	£m
Depreciation	10	10	10	10	10	10
RFCI	10	10	10	10	10	10

Applying these value drivers gives the after tax operating cash flow shown in *Table 3.2:*

Table 3.2: After tax operating cash flows

Year		1	2	3	4	5	Beyond
	£m	£m	£m	£m	£m	£m	£m
Sales Receipts	300	315.0	330.8	347.3	364.7	382.9	382.9
EBITDA		31.5	33.1	34.7	36.5	38.3	38.3
less Cash Tax		9.4	9.9	10.4	10.9	11.5	11.5
Operating Cash Flow		22.1	23.2	24.3	25.6	26.8	26.8

As indicated in the preceding section, operating cash flow does not take account of important cash outflows that will need to be incurred to support the existing and the intended sales growth. In order to achieve the intended sales growth rates, fixed and working capital investment may need to be incurred. Replacement fixed capital investment (RFCI) is required to maintain the existing assets in a satisfactory form to meet existing customer demands, whilst incremental fixed capital investment (IFCI) needs to be incurred to meet the projected sales growth rates. As we have indicated, an estimate has to be made of the amount of incremental fixed capital that will be required to support incremental sales. One way to build this in is to assume that for every £1 of sales to be generated some fixed capital investment will need to be incurred. For example, this might well be expressed as a percentage of incremental sales, such that a rate of 10% would be interpreted as for every £1 of additional sales 10 pence of incremental fixed capital investment will be required. This has to be recognised as being a rather simplistic approach insofar as investment may not occur in even increments, but may be incurred in 'lumps', however, it does represent a starting point.

Typically, there will also need to be an investment in working capital since additional sales will be difficult to sustain without incurring incremental working capital. More stock may be required and it may only be possible to achieve a growth in sales by extending credit and increasing debtors. In common with incremental fixed capital it can be assumed that for every additional £1 of sales to be generated, some working capital investment will be required. In other words, any increase in sales can only occur by taking on more stocks of raw materials and, possibly, by increasing accounts receivable (debtors). As indicated in *Table 3.1*, it is assumed that incremental fixed capital investment (IFCI) and working capital investment (WCI) will be 10% over the five year assumed planning period.

All of this can now be pulled together to estimate prospective free cash flows. These are illustrated in *Table 3.3*.

Table 3.3: From operating cash flow after tax to free cash flow

Year		1	2	3	4	5	Beyond
	£m	£m	£m	£m	£m	£m	£m
Sales Receipts	300	315.0	330.8	347.3	364.7	382.9	382.9
EBITDA		31.5	33.1	34.7	36.5	38.3	38.3
less Cash Tax		9.4	9.9	10.4	10.9	11.5	11.5
Operating Cash Flow		22.1	23.2	24.3	25.6	26.8	26.8
less RFCI		10.0	10.0	10.0	10.0	10.0	10.0
less IFCI		1.5	1.6	1.7	1.7	1.8	0.0
less IWCI		1.5	1.6	1.7	1.7	1.8	0.0
Free Cash Flow		9.1	10.0	10.9	12.2	13.2	16.8

Relationship between the different drivers of free cash flow

The relationship between the cash inflows and outflows is important to recognise. To achieve sales growth, expenditure will have to be incurred, the amount of which will depend upon the magnitude of the sales growth and the capacity of the business to expand. The interrelationship between these cash flow drivers is vital to understand. This can be seen to be so particularly in the case of the sales growth rate and incremental fixed and working capital investment. Without adequate fixed assets and working capital it may be impossible to achieve a target growth rate, let alone sustain it. However, one problem with fixed capital investment is that it may often be 'lumpy'. Beyond a certain level of production it may be impossible to produce more without investing in completely new plant and equipment. Thus, the assumption of a linear relationship between sales growth and investment is one that may not always be realistic.

The identification of key value drivers is vital and it is important to recognise that they may vary over the life cycle of a business and by type of business. In the case of the life cycle, which is illustrated in *Figure 3.1*, in the start–up phase, sales growth will often play a dominant role. However, with the development of the market and the increased participation of competitors, attention to profit margins may well be more important. This is because there will often come a point beyond which increased sales will result in value destruction, that is additional sales revenue might well be outweighed by the costs associated with generating it.

Figure 3.1: Value drivers over the life–cycle

	Stage of life cycle			
	Launch	**Growth**	**Maturity**	**Decline**
Value Drivers				
Sales Growth	Nil/High	High	Zero	Negative
EBITDA Margin	Low/High	High	Medium	Low
Cash Tax Rate	Low	Low	Standard	Depends
Fixed Capital Investment	High >>> Depreciation	High >> Depreciation	Medium/Low = or − Depreciation	Low/Reducing << Depreciation
Working Capital Investment	High	High	Low	Reducing
Cost of Capital (linked to level of business risk)	Very High	High	Medium	Low
Planning Period	Short	Medium/Long	Long	Short/Medium
Continuing Value	Large	Large	Medium	Medium

As indicated, not only will the stage of development have an impact upon the value drivers, but also the type of business. An example of this is provided in *Figure 3.2* for a systems solutions company. Work undertaken to identify the impact of the value drivers within four different businesses yielded very different results.

Figure 3.2: *Impact of value drivers within ICL (the systems solutions company)* [†]

Business	1	2	3	4
Value Drivers:				
Sales Growth Rate	Medium	High	High	Medium
EBITDA Margin	High	Medium	High	High
Cash Tax Rate	Low	Low	Low	Medium
Fixed Capital Investment	Medium	High	Low	Medium
Working Capital Investment	High	High	Medium	Medium
Cost of Capital	High	High	High	High
Planning Period	Medium	Long	Long	Long

A business like that characterised under Business 2 is dependent upon substantial fixed and working capital investment to generate sales growth. In fact, this value driver profile can be likened to a start–up situation in which fixed and working capital expenditure will be essential for stimulating future growth. It is also worth noting that in some businesses such expenditure will be directed at intangible rather than tangible items. Future growth may be driven by research and development in industries like pharmaceuticals, whilst in others expenditure on branding of products and product development may be the key.

Estimating strategic value and free cash flow

To estimate strategic value free cash flows must be discounted at the Weighted Average Cost of Capital (WACC). The WACC is the subject of *Chapter 5*. As indicated at the beginning of this chapter, such value is typically estimated by determining the value over the planning period and that from continuing period (the terminal value), which often represents the largest part of total value.

[†]   Courtesy of *Mr. I. Neill, Director of Strategic Planning, ICL plc.*

Value of the planning period

From *Table 3.1* it can be seen that the WACC has been assumed to be 10% after tax and when appropriately adjusted for inflation. This WACC represents the return required by the providers of both debt and equity finance. With knowledge of this WACC, the present value of the cash flows for the five–year planning period can be calculated, which is shown in *Table 3.4* as being £41m.

Table 3.4: Estimating strategic value

Year		1	2	3	4	5	Beyond
	£m	£m	£m	£m	£m	£m	£m
Sales Receipts	300	315.0	330.8	347.3	364.7	382.9	382.9
EBITDA		31.5	33.1	34.7	36.5	38.3	38.3
less Cash Tax		9.4	9.9	10.4	10.9	11.5	11.5
Operating Cash Flow		22.1	23.2	24.3	25.6	26.8	26.8
less RFCI		10.0	10.0	10.0	10.0	10.0	10.0
less IFCI		1.5	1.6	1.7	1.7	1.8	0.0
less IWCI		1.5	1.6	1.7	1.7	1.8	0.0
Free Cash Flow		9.1	10.0	10.9	12.2	13.2	16.8
Discount Factor		0.909	0.826	0.751	0.683	0.621	
Present Value (Free Cash Flow)		8.3	8.3	8.2	8.3	8.2	
Cumulative Present Value		8	16	25	33	41	

Estimating terminal value (TV)

A planning period of five years was used, but the issue now arises of how to estimate a Terminal Value (TV) for the continuing period beyond year 5. Assume that this company has a share price of £1 and 100 million shares. This implies a market capitalisation of £100m, while the value calculated for the five–year forecast period is £41m, a substantial difference. In fact, the value calculated represents only 41% of the market–implied value and therefore the question arises of how this difference can be accounted for. One commonly used way of estimating TV involves the calculation of a perpetuity value by dividing the assumed perpetuity cash flow by the cost of capital. For this company, the free cash flow in the continuing period beyond year 5 is £16.8m (see *Table 3.4*), which when divided by the assumed cost of capital of 10% produces a value of £168m. However, what is required is the present value of the perpetuity and not the value at the end of five years. This present value is substantially lower than £168m and is approximately £104m (£16.8m ÷ 10% x 0.621). This is obtained by discounting the £168m in five years to a present value (see *Table 3.5*).

Table 3.5: Present value of the planning period and TV

Year	1	2	3	4	5	Beyond
	£m	£m	£m	£m	£m	£m
Free Cash Flow	9.1	10.0	10.9	12.2	13.2	16.8
Discount Factor	0.909	0.826	0.751	0.683	0.621	
Present Value (Free Cash Flow)	8.3	8.3	8.2	8.3	8.2	
Cumulative Present Value	8	16	25	33	41	
Present Value of Residual Value					104	
Business Value					145	

Business value, corporate value and strategic value

To calculate a business value, the present value of the planning period has to be combined with the present value to be derived from the business beyond it. In the case of our example company, assuming a five year planning period and a cost of capital of 10%, the result is a total business value of £145m (£41m + £104m), as illustrated in *Table 3.5*. This value is now substantially higher than the market implied value of £100m, but the difference can be explained.

The business value that has been calculated is not the same as strategic value. Business value represents the value generated by the free cash flows against which all providers of funds have a claim, but strategic value is concerned with that part of business value, which is attributable to the shareholders. To understand how to arrive at this it is necessary to recall that business value was estimated by discounting the free cash flows at a cost of capital which took account of the benefit of both borrowed funds and funds provided by shareholders. To estimate strategic value the present value of borrowed funds needs to be subtracted in order to find the claim on the value of the business attributable to just the shareholders. It may also be the case that investments are held in other businesses, the benefits of which are not captured in the business valuation process. Any such benefits have to be added to determine corporate rather than business value. In fact, two adjustments are required to calculate strategic value, which take the following form:

Business value

\+   Marketable securities or investments †

\=   Corporate value

\–   Market value of debt and obligations

\=   Strategic value

÷   Number of ordinary shares

\=   Strategic value per share

For this company, the result of this calculation is shown in *Table 3.6.*

Table 3.6: Strategic value per share

Year	1	2	3	4	5	Beyond
	£m	£m	£m	£m	£m	£m
Free Cash Flow	9.1	10.0	10.9	12.2	13.2	16.8
Discount Factor	0.909	0.826	0.751	0.683	0.621	
Present Value (Free Cash Flow)	8.3	8.3	8.2	8.3	8.2	
Cumulative Present Value	8	16	25	33	41	
Present Value of Residual Value					104	
Business Value					145	

Year	1	2	3	4	5	Beyond
	£m	£m	£m	£m	£m	£m
Business Value					145	
add Marketable Securities					0	
Corporate Value					145	
less Market Value of Debt					20	
Strategic Value					125	
Number of Shares (m)					100	
Strategic Value Per Share					£1.25	

---

†   Surplus cash invested in marketable securities (non operating assets) are assumed to create no additional value, i.e. their net present value is zero

The estimated business value is £145m, there are no marketable securities (e.g. interest earning deposits), and the value of debt is £20m. Debt and obligations are deducted from corporate value, resulting in £125m. The number of ordinary shares (assumed to be 100 million then divides this) and a strategic value per share of £1.25 is obtained.

How might the figure for strategic value be interpreted? The company has a current share price of £1.00. As implied earlier, this share price can be compared with the publicly quoted price determined by the forces of demand and supply, to see if a value gap exists. This is the term applied to the difference between the publicly quoted share price and estimates of its value using specific company information. For the company, there is a value gap of £0.25 at a 10% cost of capital (£1.25 – £1.00).

What does this strategic value per share represent? It is the estimated value per share and it is very dependent upon the assumptions made about the key value drivers. Change any of these and so too does the value. For example, an increase in the EBITDA margin, ceteris paribus, will result in a higher strategic value per share. By way of illustration, in one company that was analysed using this framework, an increase in the EBITDA margin to the levels currently achieved by peer group companies, had the effect of doubling the strategic value per share and formed part of the rationale for it becoming an acquisition target.

Let us pause at this point and reflect upon the figure for strategic value estimated for the company. It represents the value derived from a fairly simplistic view of the company. In reality, it would be reasonable to expect that estimates used in a full valuation would have to involve considerable detailed analysis. For example, many businesses provide multiple services and/or produce multiple products. For them, a more realistic process of valuation would be to calculate the cash flows relevant to, say, each business unit using planning periods that reflect the different distinctive capabilities of each, and then to discount them at a required rate of return relevant to each unit. All of these individual values could then be aggregated and the strategic value estimated. The ability to be able to go into such detail depends upon information being available. Obtaining information can often be difficult, but a guide as to what may be available is provided in *Figure 3.3*.

Figure 3.3: Possible sources of available information

| | | Internal | | External | |
		Past	Future	Past	Future
Financial	**Numeric**	Management Accounting	Budgets and Forecasts	Competitors' Results	Broker's Forecasts
	Text	Results Narrative	Five year plan	Brokers' View	Press Opinion
Non–financial	**Numeric**	Operating Performance	Capacity Planning	Market Share	Market Research
	Text	Performance Commentary	Strategic Goals	Trade media	Technology Forecasts

Source: Accountancy Age, 6 March 1997

Summary checklist

- Five value drivers enable a free cash flow picture of a business to be generated.

- This free cash flow picture is generated over a planning period, the sixth value driver, beyond which a terminal value may be calculated for the continuing period.

- A seventh value driver, the cost of capital (often referred to as WACC), is essential for converting cash flows into values. (This is covered in its own right in *Chapter 5*)

- Robust valuations require that the nature of the interrelationship between all seven value drivers is consistent.

- The framework for estimating Strategic Value is very effective in forcing clarity of thought about tough issues that drive the value of a business and to help to organise thought around the limitations imposed by having imperfect data.

Chapter 4

Assessing Competitive Advantage

Chapter preview

- The critical issues involved in estimating over what period of time (planning period) cash flows should be forecast.

- The link between the value of a business captured during this planning period and beyond it (the continuing period).

- The use of strategic frameworks as a starting point to ensure that the right questions are asked in relation to the length of the planning period used.

- How the planning period may be estimated in practice by first looking at a Price Earnings interpretation, and secondly, by using the concept of the market implied duration.

- The dynamic interrelationship between the planning period, the competitive advantage period and the terminal value.

Competitive Advantage Period (CAP)

In our experience, the most important challenge in creating value is to understand that it is about having and maintaining a competitive advantage. What the shareholder value methods like free cash flow permit is the measurement of value, making it happen is quite another matter. As we will illustrate, the challenge is to be better than the competition in some way, such that the goods and services provided have a higher perceived value to customers. The same is also arguably true for the perceived value of the shares to shareholders.

How the value of a business can be estimated using the free cash flow approach focusing upon a number of key value drivers was demonstrated in *Chapter 3*. This value consisted of that from the planning period and an assumed period beyond, known as the continuing period. The value from the continuing period, the terminal value, represents 72% (£104 ÷ £145) of the total corporate value and, as such, the size of this proportion typically represents a major cause for concern. If the time horizon is extended this proportion falls, but this then raises the million–dollar question – 'how far out to go?' The length of the planning period, together with the issue of competitive advantage and the Competitive Advantage Period (CAP), that period over which a firm enjoys a competitive advantage, are the subject of this chapter. Before this discussion, it is useful for us to try and define competitive advantage and to put it into context with the other main area for consideration in the next chapter, the cost of capital.

One simple starting point for understanding competitive advantage is that it is achieved when the economic return on capital is greater than the cost of that capital. Imagine you run a successful business that has achieved a competitive advantage because of the reputation you have developed. The result should be that you will be achieving an economic return on the capital invested over and above the cost of that capital. New entrants will be attracted to your market, such that if you do not sustain the achieved returns your competitive advantage will be eroded. Without effort to sustain this competitive advantage, your return could fall such that you only achieve an economic return equal to the cost of the capital invested or, even worse, below. As you will see, this thinking is developed in terms of trying to assess the Competitive Advantage Period, but information is also required about the cost of capital. The cost of capital can be seen as a benchmark against which to assess the economic return on capital invested, hence we need to have some understanding of its estimation.

Relationship between CAP and terminal value (TV)

As will be illustrated, there is often confusion between the planning period and the CAP, and the two are not necessarily the same. In reality, most valuation models use a planning period over which it is assumed that a return on capital is earned in excess of the cost of capital.

Figure 4.1: Relationship between planning period and terminal value

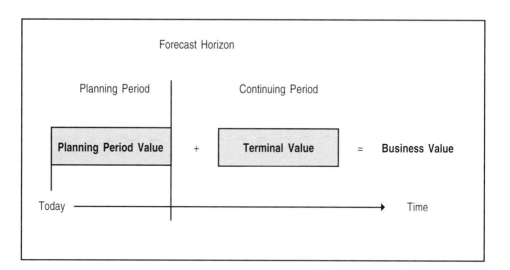

As illustrated in the example in the last chapter, a common approach is to forecast over a finite time period, like five years, and then to capture any remaining value assumed to arise in a perpetuity calculation. The logic behind this is that once the market has been established, cash receipts can be viewed as being potentially indefinite, as long as necessary replacement investment in fixed assets or other areas, like marketing or research and development expenditure, is undertaken to maintain existing position. The use of a perpetuity calculation is convenient because it means that cash flows do not have to be estimated forever. However, blind reliance upon a standard period for assessing free cash flows and the adoption of a perpetuity calculation to capture value thereafter is inadequate. It is essential to look for ways of capturing future value as realistically as possible and to recognise that different business units may well have different time horizons over which they need to consider their long term strategic plans. The CAP is yet another variable in any valuation and can be considered to be a vital issue to assess. Unfortunately, whilst the principle underpinning its importance is understood, its estimation in practice is not. Quite simply, this is because its assessment is based upon a good deal of qualitative judgement and it is difficult to be accurate in its determination. Often less energy is expended in its determination than with other issues, which fall more readily within the financial specialist's comfort zone and, unfortunately, there are no easy answers to this issue about what is an appropriate CAP. Certainly, this chapter does not suggest a simple solution, but it does offer some guidelines based upon both theory and practice.

The Competitive Advantage Period (CAP) and strategic theory

As indicated, the CAP is the time during which a company is expected to generate returns on incremental investment that exceeds its cost of capital. Economic theory suggests that competitive forces will eventually drive returns down to the cost of capital over time. In other words, if a company earns returns above the cost of capital, it will attract competitors into the industry, the consequence of which will be a reduction in industry returns.

The concept of CAP is not new and has existed in the finance literature for many years, although not necessarily under that name. It has been labelled variously, examples of which are 'value growth duration' and 'T' [36,37,38]. For example, it was formalised by *Miller and Modigliani* through their seminal work on valuation [39].

A number of strategic approaches that will be reviewed in the following sections have been developed that can, in principle, be applied to determine the length of the competitive advantage period.

Understanding the external context

One approach commonly quoted within the context of business valuation is that associated with the 'five forces' framework developed by *Michael Porter* [40]. The competitive period can be explained using five forces identified by *Porter* and illustrated in *Figure 4.2*.

Figure 4.2: Porters' five forces

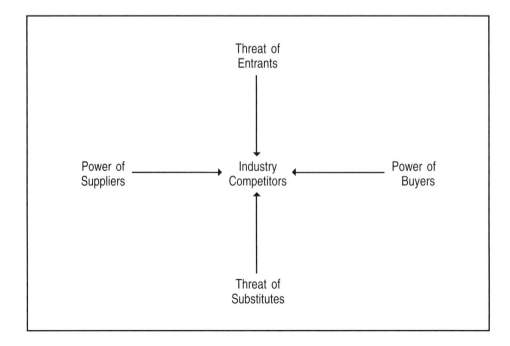

A company's competitive advantage may be threatened by potential entrants on the one hand and the possibility of substitute products on the other. It will also be affected by the relative power of suppliers and buyers and by the degree of competitive rivalry within the industry in which it exists.

In establishing the length of the competitive advantage period, a company's management needs to be aware of these forces. It may be aware of certain potential entrants to the market but it may also know that the barriers to entry are such that it will take a new entrant to the industry four or five years before it becomes a serious threat. Similarly, it may be aware that in the market from which it buys its most important raw materials, mergers and takeovers are taking place, which will make the suppliers' market less competitive and raw materials more expensive. Again, it is a question of judging the length of time over which the suppliers' prices will rise.

Although the contribution by *Porter* has been invaluable, there has been considerable interest in terms of what makes firms that operate within the same industry different. There is evidence to suggest that the performance achieved by an organisation depends more upon its relative performance within an industry rather than the industry sector in which it operates. For example, *Rumelt* analysed the returns of a large sample of American firms by reference to their profitability in different industries [41]. *Rumelt's* findings are summarised in *Table 4.1*.

Table 4.1: Contributions to variance of profits across business units

	%
Corporate ownership	0.8
Industry effects	8.3
Cyclical effects	7.8
Business unit specific effects	46.4
Unexplained factors [†]	36.7

By far the largest contributor to explaining differences in profits is business unit–specific effects, which account for 46.4% of the contribution to variance of profits. In other words, there are no systematically successful firms or industries, but there are systematically successful business units. These are the businesses that enjoy competitive advantages and outperform their competitors year by year.

---

† Sometimes referred to as the 'X' factor.

The *Rumelt* evidence, therefore, suggests that the performance achieved by an organisation depends more upon its relative performance within an industry than the industry itself [42]. In other words, good relative performance within an industry translates into the generation of superior returns. Further work in this area has stimulated the view that this relative performance relates to core (distinctive) capabilities that can give businesses an edge.

Analysis of the internal context

Porter also outlined a framework for value chains [43]. The underlying principle of this framework is that all tasks performed by a business organisation can be classified into 9 broad categories:

● Five primary activities: inbound logistics, operations, outbound logistics, marketing, sales and service, plus

● Four support activities: firm infrastructure, human resource management, technology development and procurement.

Many adaptations of the value chain framework have emerged over time. One potentially useful variant is illustrated in *Figure 4.3*.

Figure 4.3: Value chain

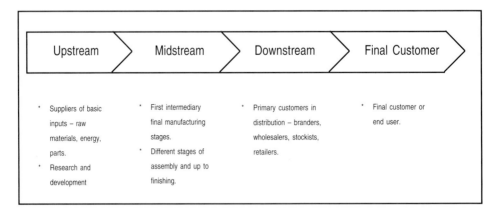

Since the value chain is composed of the set of activities performed by a business, it provides an effective way to diagnose the position of a business against its major competitors. Using the approach, it is possible to define the foundation for actions aimed at sustaining a competitive advantage, as opposed to the forces which determine industry attractiveness to the business. The latter are largely external and uncontrollable by the firm, whereas the activities within the value chain framework constitute the foundation of the controllable factors to achieve competitive superiority.

Research by *Kay* has identified four types of distinctive capability [44]:

1.   Reputation.

2.   Architecture.

3.   Innovation.

4.   Strategic assets.

Reputation,

Enables a company to charge higher prices, or gain larger market share at a competitive price, for a functionally equivalent product. Examples of companies quoted by *Kay* for whom reputation is important are *Lloyds TSB* and *Sainsbury's,* the UK food retailing supermarket chain.

Architecture

Can be viewed in terms of a unique structure of relationships in or around the company that is between the company and its suppliers. Via the development of a strategic architecture, an organisation should be able to commit the technical and production linkages across business units which will build upon distinct skills and capabilities that, cannot be matched or easily replicated by other organisations. Examples of companies held as having strategic architecture as a distinctive capability are *Marks and Spencer* and *Benetton.*

Innovation

Is seen as being a very strong source of competitive advantage, but one that is difficult to sustain because of the potential for replication. Patent protection can play an important part in reaping the benefits from innovation, but may be difficult to achieve in practice. One noteworthy exploiter of this approach has been the pharmaceuticals industry.

Strategic Assets

Ownership of strategic assets, differs from the others because it is the product of the market or regulatory environment rather than of a company's distinctive achievement. An example is a concession to exploit a resource or an exclusive right to supply as a product of the market, or regulatory environment [†].

These four distinctive capabilities can also be seen in terms of the core competency approach associated with *Prahalad and Hamel* [45]. This focused upon the development of a strategic architecture to identify and commit the technical and production linkages across business units so as to build upon distinct skills and capabilities that cannot be matched or easily replicated by other organisations.

---

†   Associated with this grouping may be many distinctive capabilities often overlooked, like those associated with the skill of the workforce.

These competencies can be thought of as being the collective learning of the organisation, particularly how to coordinate diverse production skills and integrate multiple streams of technology. Because of diversified information systems, patterns of communications, managerial rewards and so on, there will be an inevitable fragmentation of core competencies and an impetus for learning will be required.

In principle, *Kay's* four distinctive capabilities should enable an organisation to achieve what are often regarded as being major sources of competitive advantage – size, market share, market selection, and market position. However, they will continue to add value only if their capability and distinctiveness are sustainable. In fact, one key issue *Kay* considered was the sustainability of these four distinctive capabilities. On the basis of his research, *Kay* suggested reputation as generally being the easiest to sustain, strategic assets as being sustainable over long periods only if there are no changes in regulation or market conditions, and innovation as being the most difficult. In fact, some specific sources of sustainable competitive advantage were identified in research by *Aaker* (see *Table 4.2*), who considered what the managers of 248 distinct businesses oriented towards service and hitech businesses thought were the sustainable competitive advantages of their businesses [46]. He found that sustainable sources of competitive advantage varied from business to business and arose from more than one source. This indicates that it is not sufficient for a business to base its strategy on a single source of competitive advantage and that the challenge for both management and investors is to be able to identify the sources for any given business. What is more, and is so often overlooked, is that identifiable sources of competitive advantage do not necessarily translate into a CAP for valuation purposes. For there to be a CAP for such purposes, there has to be sustainability. If a firm cannot sustain its competitive advantage, then by definition it will be unable to generate future returns in excess of the cost of capital, quite simply because others will be able to enter the market and erode excess returns.

Table 4.2: Sustainable competitive advantages in 248 businesses [47]

		Hightech	Service	Other	Total
1	Reputation for Quality	26	50	29	105
2	Customer Service/Product Support	23	40	15	78
3	Name Recognition/High Profile	8	42	21	71
4	Retain Good Management & Engineering Staff	17	43	5	65
5	Low Cost Production	17	15	21	53
6	Financial Resources	11	26	14	51
7	Customer Orientation/Feedback Market Research	13	26	9	48
8	Product Line Breadth	11	25	17	47
9	Technical Superiority	30	7	9	46
10	Installed Base of Satisfied Customers	19	22	4	45
11	Segmentation/Focus	7	22	16	45
12	Product Characteristics/Differentiation	12	15	10	37
13	Continuing Production Innovation	15	20	10	35
14	Market Share	12	14	9	35
15	Size/Location of Distribution	10	12	13	34
16	Low-Price/High-Value Offering	6	20	6	32
17	Knowledge of Business	2	25	4	31
18	Pioneer/Early Entrant in Industry	11	11	6	28
19	Efficient, Flexible Production/Operations Adaptable to Customers	4	17	4	26
20	Effective Sales Force	10	9	4	23
21	Overall Marketing Skills	7	9	7	23
22	Shared Vision/Culture	5	13	4	22
23	Strategic Goals	6	7	9	22
24	Powerful Well-Known Parent	7	7	6	20
25	Location	0	10	10	20
26	Effective Advertising/Image	5	6	6	17
27	Enterprising/Entrepreneurial	4	3	6	11
28	Good Co-ordination	3	2	5	10
29	Engineering Research Development	8	2	0	10
30	Short-term Planning	2	1	5	8
31	Good Distributor Relations	2	4	1	7
32	Other	6	20	5	31
	Total	322	552	283	1157
	Number of Businesses	68	113	67	248
	Average Number of Sustainable Competitive Advantages	4.73	4.88	4.22	4.65

Introducing the dynamic of time through life cycles

Other sources of the potential underpinnings of CAP can also be found in the literature. For example, *Williams* has extended the *Porter* framework by incorporating the time dimension into value chain analysis. He has classified industry environments into three types [48].

- Class I industries, characterised by competitively stable value chains, which over time are relatively unchanged.

- Class II industries, characterised by smoothly evolving value chains, which are reinforced through scale based learning.

- Class III industries, characterised by dynamic and unstable value chains, which accelerate rapidly to maturity.

In an alternative view of the product life cycle *Ansoff* argued for an approach that considers the need provided by a product rather than the product itself [49]. This equates with looking at a demand life cycle, capturing ongoing, changing levels of need. Such needs are satisfied by technology and *Ansoff* used 'calculating power' as an example of a need that has existed for thousands of years. The changing level of need is represented by a demand life cycle, so in terms of calculating power, the need was initially met by using fingers (as reflected in the Arabic numeric system); then by abacuses; later by slide rules; then mechanical adding machines; electronic calculators; and currently by computers. Each technological development offered enhanced benefits such as speed, cost, capacity, or increased facilities. *Ansoff* suggested these to be demand technology cycles, with an 'S' shaped format suggesting emergence, rapid growth, slower growth, maturity and finally decline.

Within each demand technology cycle there will be a succession of product forms that satisfy the specific need at the time. *Ansoff* used the hand calculator as an example. Initially, it took the form of a large plastic box with a small screen and numerical operating keys. Its performance was limited to four tasks – addition, subtraction, multiplication and division. This was soon superseded by smaller hand held calculators performing many more mathematical and scientific functions. These in turn were succeeded by yet smaller versions and at much lower costs.

These cycles in the development of calculators suggests some interesting implications. If a company concentrates its product development, research and development and marketing efforts in a narrow aspect of the overall cycle, it may miss the opportunity to expand its market base. What is more, it may also overlook the fact that the demand technology cycle may be facing obsolescence. Companies need to decide in which demand technology to invest and when to move into a new technology. For some companies in some industries the choice is difficult as the demand technology cycles tend to have very short effective life spans, while others may become obsolescent very slowly and merge with the next generation. This means that in reality, CAP decisions may be very complex.

Whilst it is widely acknowledged that products go through cycles, it is not well recognised that business designs also go through cycles and reach obsolescence. A business design refers to the totality of how a company selects its customers, defines and differentiates its offerings, defines the tasks it will perform itself and those it will outsource, configures its resources, goes to market, create utility for customers, and captures profit. *Slywotzky* has adopted the term value migration to illustrate that a business design can exist in only one of three states: value inflow, stability and value outflow [50]. These states emphasise the importance of relative value creation power, with a view to satisfying customer priorities better than competitors, thereby earning superior returns. More specifically, these three states are:

● Value inflow. In the initial phase, a company starts to absorb value from other parts of its industry because its business design proves superior in satisfying customer priorities. *Microsoft* and *EDS* are among companies currently reckoned to be experiencing the value inflow phase.

● Stability. This is characterised by business designs that are well matched to customer priorities and by overall competitive equilibrium. Companies such as *Dupont* are considered to be in this phase.

● Value outflow. In the third phase, value starts to move away from an organisation's traditional activities towards business designs that meet evolving customer priorities more effectively.

Figure 4.4: Three stages of value migration

Value migration among business designs takes place at different levels:

● between industries, e.g. telecommunications, entertainment and computer

● between companies in the same industry, e.g. *BT, Energis, Vodaphone, Cellnet*, etc.

● within a single company, e.g. fixed lines, mobile, multimedia

---

Focusing upon value migration at the industry level is a useful first step because it creates a context in which to evaluate individual business designs. It's not that value disappears, but that it moves – rapidly at times – towards new activities and skills, and toward new business designs whose superiority in meeting customer priorities makes profit possible. To meet the challenge of value migration, managers must ask, 'Where in my industry can a profit be made? How is that changing? What is driving that change? What can my organisation do about it?' Beneath these questions lies a more fundamental inquiry – 'What is the changing pattern of what customers need, want and are willing to pay for, and what business designs respond most effectively to this changing pattern?' In every industry there is a limited set of key moves that allows advantage to be taken of the next cycle of value growth. Every business design has a limited value creation life–cycle. Managers must act to create the next viable business design. The key questions are – 'Which move should I make? What future business design element will be most important? What future competitors do I have to worry about most?' This is where scenarios (reviewed in *Chapter 2*) can be a very useful tool for helping to answer these questions.

Figure 4.5: Summary of strategic perspectives relevant to the CAP

Three broad areas of focus	Strategic tools
Understanding the external context within which a business operates, and performance relative to others within the industry.	Porter's Five forces for industry analysis.
Analysis of the internal activities that comprise businesses and sources of sustainable competitive advantage.	Value chain of activities, distinctive capabilities and core competencies.
Synthesis of the external and internal perspective through the introduction of the dynamic of time and business as a game in a constantly evolving landscape and changing rules.	Life cycle analysis of products and technology. Three stages of value migration for industries and businesses.

Estimating CAP in practice

In determining CAP in practice, the assumption used about the time horizon will have a significant impact upon the size of any Terminal Value (TV). TV, that value arising from the beyond the assumed CAP, known as the 'continuing period', is often a source of considerable concern in many valuations. This is important because it frequently accounts for a significant proportion of total value. In fact, in some circumstances, like a start up or a development in a new market, it may account for nearly all of the total value. A good real–life example of this was the valuation of the UK telecommunications company, *Orange plc* and which was floated in 1996. Initial value estimates for the business in excess of £2.8bn were produced by a number of analysts, of which £2.0bn was the result of a terminal value estimate beyond a 10 year forecast period for free cash flows[†].

[†] A similar observation regarding the potential contribution from the terminal value was also confirmed by *McKinsey and Company*, which demonstrated that over an eight–year forecast period the terminal value in four industries accounted for anywhere between 56 percent to 125 percent of total value.

Research has revealed that five years is popular as a planning period estimate for many UK companies [51]. When compared crudely alongside market PE multiples of between 17 and 19 years on current after tax earnings attributable to shareholders, there is the potential for a 'value gap'. One way of preventing a value gap is for a longer–term planning period to be used, but this raises the immediate concern that planning for just five years can often be difficult enough. The fact that management looks typically only to a limited future period, say five years, is the real problem and there should be explicit recognition that the continuing period and the terminal value associated with it as being something directly within management's control. It is not a residual, but one of the most critical parts of the 'value future'. As such, it needs to be owned and actively managed, even though it may deal with a time horizon too distant to analyse prescriptively. If the valuation of this time period is seen to relate to the selected planning period, it is much more than a passive residual. In fact, it can be looked upon as being the consequence of actions taken over the time period falling within the comfort zone of management action.

Approaches for dealing with the CAP (and hence the terminal value) rely upon estimating Market Implied CAP (MICAP) and applying scenario thinking. Scenario thinking was covered in *Chapter 2* and its intention in this context is to try to ensure that short– and long–term pressures upon the business environment are not overlooked. While this approach is invaluable in freeing thinking, the all important question arises, 'is it possible to estimate CAP empirically? This will now be considered with reference to the estimation of MICAP.

Market Implied CAP (MICAP)

This approach can be thought of as involving the following steps [52]. First, a proxy for unbiased market expectations of six value drivers (other than CAP) is required, assuming use of a seven value driver model, i.e. sales growth rate, operating profit margin, cash tax rate, fixed capital needs, working capital needs, cost of capital and CAP. Second, a valuation model is built, including a terminal value calculation based upon an assumed perpetuity. Last, the time period over which the forecast is undertaken is 'stretched' as many years as is necessary to achieve the company's current market price for its shares, i.e. the period over which the return on new investment stays above WACC is stretched to achieve the market capitalisation. The resulting time period is the assumed CAP.

There is a belief that lengthening the CAP in this way can help to explain the 'X' factor [†], and a good illustration of this has been provided by *Mauboussin and Johnson* [53]. Based upon a study of a selection of companies within the packaged food industry in the September 1982 to August 1989 period, they found using the approach described above that the CAP for this group roughly doubled in the seven–year period. In fact, this time period corresponded with most companies streamlining their business portfolios, cutting costs, increasing vital marketing expenditure, and increasing cash flows.

[†]   Unexplained factors in *Rumelt's* research, see *Table 4.1*

Whilst this approach is useful as a practical tool, particularly from the perspective of the external analyst, it does have some limitations, that may be summarised as follows:

● It presupposes that the market price of the share is an appropriate reflection of future prospects, but there may be a radical shift in prospect that has not been detected by the market. Many acquisitions have been concerned with business transformations not reflected in the share price until the occurrence of a predatory move.

● What happens when there is no share price, e.g. for a private company or division/business unit? In this case there is no share price against which to 'stretch'. In our experience this can be dealt with effectively by undertaking market implied duration stretch on a carefully selected set of peer group companies, combined with scenario analysis.

Interrelationship between the planning period, the CAP and the terminal value

As mentioned in the introduction to this chapter there are no easy answers to what is an appropriate CAP, in fact any decisions concerning the CAP cannot be taken in isolation. As *Figure 4.6* shows, the planning period adopted is related to the CAP which, in turn, is related to the terminal value calculation. Similarly, the terminal value calculation used makes certain assumptions regarding the CAP that, in turn, influences the planning period chosen.

Figure 4.6: Dynamic interrelationship between planning period, CAP and terminal value

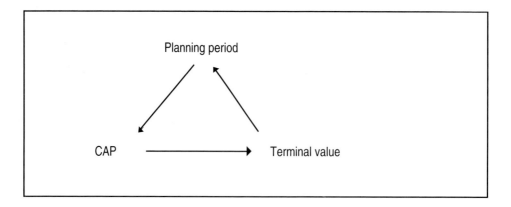

Two practical possibilities exist for the relationship between the planning period and the CAP:

● First, the planning period is equal to the CAP, which implies that there is no new value created beyond it because the returns on new capital have fallen to the cost of capital.

● Second, the planning period is less than the CAP and hence there is new value being created beyond it that needs to be captured by the valuation. As will be illustrated in the next chapter, there are alternative possible approaches that can be used to take account of this additional value.

Summary checklist

● A critical determinant of any valuation is what period of time should be used for the planning period.

● Literature from strategic theory provides the starting point for understanding what could be the underlying determinants of the CAP.

● A securities market–based perspective of the CAP can be derived using the seven value driver framework to ascertain what is implied by the markets.

● From an internal perspective scenario thinking is invaluable in understanding what may underpin the CAP.

● It is important to make explicit assumptions about whether the planning period used in any valuation is the CAP and, if the two are not the same, what will be the implications for the valuation, in particular the terminal value.

● Pragmatism dictates that crosschecking results, using a number of different approaches, may assist in gaining a deeper understanding of the CAP.

Chapter 5

Terminal Value and the Cost of Capital

Chapter preview

- The principles and potential application of the three different approaches that can be used to calculate Terminal Value (TV):

  1. Discounted Cash Flow (DCF).

  2. Market relative valuation.

  3. Asset valuation.

- The contribution that the perpetuity approach can make in challenging valuation assumptions.

- The important interrelationship between the TV and the planning period chosen.

- The importance of the Weighted Average Cost of Capital (WACC) as the benchmark to be used to assess whether value is created or not for the providers of capital to a business.

- How to calculate the WACC using a three step process, which involves calculating the cost of equity, the cost of debt and estimating the target capital structure.

- How to calculate the cost of equity using the Capital Asset Pricing Model (CAPM), and how to calculate the cost of debt.

- Issues involved in estimating the cost of capital from a business unit perspective.

Introduction

The Terminal Value (TV), and some of the approaches, like the perpetuity method, that can be used in its estimation were introduced in *Chapter 3*. As illustrated, this value which arises from the continuing period, is often a source of considerable concern because it accounts for a significant proportion of total value.

In view of the potential significance of the TV in any decision, the structure illustrated in *Figure 5.1* can be used to guide the assessment and selection of an appropriate method, and its estimation.

Figure 5.1:   Selecting an appropriate TV method

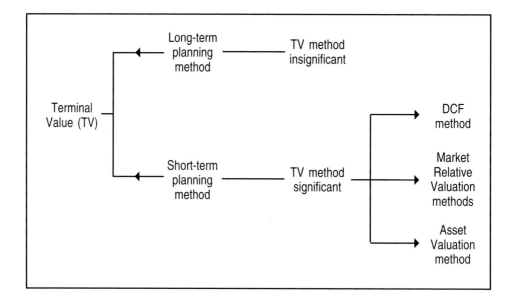

The starting point illustrated in *Figure 5.1* is consideration of the time period. If the time period under consideration is very long, say in excess of 20 years, as may be the case of valuing a concession, then the TV estimation is relatively insignificant. For example, the value of £1 in year 20 is 0.149, assuming a discount rate of 10%. This means that the relative importance of the TV to the total value becomes insignificant over such periods, by comparison with frequently used short–term time periods, like five years. In year five at 10% the discount rate is 0.621, meaning that every TV £ counts substantially towards the total value.

In the case of a short–term time horizon being used, TV and the choice of a method, for its calculation become important. Methods that can be used for estimating TV when a short–term view is taken are shown in *Figure 5.1* as:

● Discounted Cash Flow (DCF).

● Market Relative Valuation Methods.

● Asset Valuation.

Discounted Cash Flow (DCF) Methods

As illustrated in *Figure 5.2*, a number of issues have to be taken into consideration in estimating a TV using DCF analysis.

Figure 5.2: Issues in estimating TV using Discounted Cash Flow methods

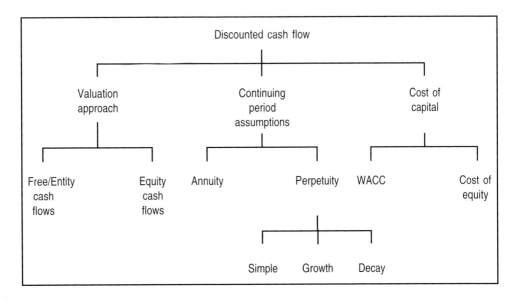

The way in which a DCF TV is estimated will be influenced by the:

● valuation approach(es) adopted;

● continuing period assumptions;

● cost of capital.

Many of these issues are interrelated. For example, as illustrated with reference to *Omega plc* in *Chapter 3*, DCF TVs can be calculated from a free cash flow figure, or a Strategic Value Added (economic profit) number as will be illustrated in *Chapter 6*. The end result of using these two alternative valuation approaches can be shown to be the same in the world of ceteris paribus (other things equal) assumptions, although in our experience in practice this is rarely so. What is more, irrespective of the valuation method adopted, there will still be choices to be made about the assumptions for the planning period and the continuing period beyond.

Perpetuity TV Valuations

As illustrated in *Chapter 3*, many proponents of DCF valuation methods use perpetuity TV calculations. There are different perpetuity methods that can be used which, in simple terms, assume that:

● only the cost of capital can be earned in the continuing period, or

● more can be earned than the cost of capital, or

● less can be earned than the cost of capital.

To correspond with these choices, the following TV calculations can be used:

● Simple perpetuity.

● Perpetuity with growth.

● Perpetuity with decay.

Simple perpetuity

The simple perpetuity approach is often represented as assuming constant cash flows beyond the planning period. It can be thought of as being reliant upon the same principles as those associated with calculating an annuity, but instead we consider a special case in which constant free cash flows are assumed to be received for an infinite rather than a finite period [†].

The simple perpetuity TV is typically calculated as follows:

$$\text{Terminal Value} \quad = \quad \frac{FCF_{T+1}}{WACC}$$

Where,

FCF_{T+1} =   Normalised free cash flow for the continuing period

$WACC$ =   Weighted Average Cost of Capital

[†] The simple perpetuity can be derived from the growing free cash flow perpetuity formula (discussed in the next section). For now, it is important to stress that the simple perpetuity does not mean that growth will necessarily be zero, rather it indicates that any growth will add nothing to value, because the return associated with growth will equal only the cost of capital. In other words, it reflects the fact that the cash flows resulting from future investments will not affect the value of the firm, because the overall rate of return earned on them will only equal the cost of capital – hence the method is often referred to as the 'convergence formula'.

For *Omega plc*, the free cash flow in the continuing period beyond year 5 is £16.8m (see *Table 3.4*). Assuming this to be the normalised free cash flow and when divided by the assumed cost of capital of 10%, the result is a value of approximately £168m. However, this is not the value required for purposes of undertaking most valuations. Typically what is needed is the present value of the perpetuity and not the value at the end of five years. This present value is substantially lower than £168m and is in fact £104m (£16.8m ÷ 10% x 0.621), i.e. £168m to received in five years discounted to a present value.

Perpetuity with growth

There may be circumstances like the valuation of a telecommunications business in which it is believed that it will be possible to earn a return above the cost of capital in the continuing period. In such circumstances the perpetuity with growth approach is often argued as being more appropriate. It can be calculated as follows:

$$\text{Terminal Value} = \frac{FCF_{T+1}}{WACC - g}$$

Where,

FCF_{T+1}	=	Normalised free cash flow for the continuing period
WACC	=	Weighted Average Cost of Capital
g	=	Expected growth in free cash flow into perpetuity

Assuming a growth in free cash flow into perpetuity of 2% results in the following TV estimate:

$$= \text{£16.8m} \div (0.10 - 0.02)$$

$$= \text{£210m}$$

Assuming a perpetuity growth rate of 2%, the resulting TV is £210m, 25% higher than using the simple perpetuity. Clearly, the growth rate used has a significant impact upon the TV and overall value and it is important to be able to justify the rate selected. An example of the use of perpetuity with growth assumptions and its justification can be seen with reference to the UK telecommunications company *Orange plc*. The rationale for the use of the approach was that within the UK market growth forecasts for the mobile industry had been substantially underestimated. In the advertising campaign, which preceded the award of the two mobile licences for the UK market in 1983, *Cellnet's* market forecast was for 100,000 subscribers while *Vodafone's* estimate was 250,000 for the total market! Today, the UK cellular base consists of about 6 million subscribers and forecasts for the market out to the year 2001 range from 10 million to 18 million. In fact, some manufacturers estimated the eventual penetration of mobile phones at 1.2 per person. The rationale behind such forecasts was that buying the service and the handset need not be linked and handsets may well be as cheap as digital watches in due course.

This approach has to be used cautiously because of the impact of growth assumptions on total value. In the case of a belief in real growth opportunities existing in the market, a reality check is essential. This reality check could be as simple as calculating what volumes would be say 10 to 20 years ahead, based upon such a growth rate and making comparisons with the total potential market, competitive forces, and the like. It is also worth noting that perpetuity with growth calculations are sometimes used to take account of inflation. The assumption is that the cash flows in the continuing period should grow at a rate in perpetuity that reflects the inflation rate. Essentially, the logic of this is that if the free cash flow used in the continuing period calculation is not assumed to grow at the rate of inflation, it represents a real number that should be discounted at a real number. Given that WACC in the formula is expressed in nominal terms, conversion to a real rate is achieved by deducting expected inflation as g from the denominator. Opinion is divided about such practice in its use. Those who favour it do so because it is consistent with general principles, i.e. real cash flows should be discounted at a real rate. Those who dislike it argue (amongst other points) that it is more realistic to assume that any growth will probably require at least additional working capital expenditure, and that replacement (maintenance) fixed capital investment is likely to exceed depreciation.

Perpetuity with decay

This is a very conservative approach, which can be thought of as a special case of the perpetuity with growth method, i.e. growth is negative in perpetuity. It assumes that after the planning period the company will be unable to earn even its cost of capital and in terms of the perpetuity with growth formula discussed earlier, it is calculated as follows:

$$\text{Terminal Value} = \frac{FCF_{T+1}}{WACC - (-g)}$$

Assuming a negative growth in free cash flow into perpetuity of 3% results in the following TV estimate for *Omega plc*:

$$= \text{£16.8m} \div (0.10 - (-0.03))$$

$$= \text{£129m}$$

Assuming a decay rate of 3% the result is a substantial reduction in the TV from the simple perpetuity. However, by implication the circumstances under which such conditions would prevail would suggest an exit strategy as being appropriate, in which case an asset–based valuation basis would often be argued as being more appropriate.

Key Issues in Estimating Terminal Value Using the Perpetuity Approach

TV is often the largest contributor to total value when using a perpetuity calculation, and a relatively short planning period. The further into the future that the planning period extends, the lower is the relative contribution made by the continuing period. For example, over a five–year planning period results similar to *Omega plc* are not uncommon, on average, where TV represents 60–70% of total value. Over a ten-year period this will often switch, with 30–40% of total value coming from the TV. The underlying message is that it is desirable to project as far forward as possible with the planning period, but this is often counter to the planning period culture within many companies [54]. This tends to mean the adoption of relatively short planning periods and perpetuity TV calculations is not uncommon. However, there can be seen as being good justification for using the perpetuity approach even under such circumstances. The reason is best understood with reference to the following questions that can be used with executives involved in reviewing the strategic value of their business for the first time:

1. 'Do you believe your business has a life in excess of the planning period you adopt?' The response to this is typically yes.

2. Would it not be a good idea to use a period longer than your current planning period?' The answer is typically yes, but it would not be worth the effort because of the highly speculative nature of forecasting over long time periods.

3. 'Do you have faith in your planning period assumptions and numbers?' The result is typically a reserved yes, with greatest confidence being felt with earlier rather than later numbers.

Given such yes responses there is a good case for using the perpetuity approach as a starting point, based upon their numbers from the planning period. The advantage of this approach is that it relates long–term value to assumptions about business potential based upon managerial judgement and insight. In fact, reflection upon this approach by managers usually prompts the observation that the TV according to this approach is dependent upon their assumptions about the time period in which they have greatest comfort and the other value drivers, not least of which is the cost of capital.

Important Considerations in Applying DCF Approaches

1. All DCF methods are heavily dependent upon expected future cash flow estimates and estimates for the cost of capital. Given this, the approach is easiest to accept for companies where cash flows are currently positive and can be estimated with some reliability for future periods and for which a proxy for risk that can be used to obtain discount rates is available. The problem is that they often represent the only practical alternative for companies with quite the opposite characteristics.

2. DCF TV calculations should really reflect a company's business cycle. With

this in mind it is important to forecast far enough out to capture a complete business cycle and to use normalised figures as the input into the TV formula. Industry dependence on macroeconomic conditions typically differs in different stages of the business cycle and it is important to recognise that TV estimates are particularly sensitive to the phase of the cycle on which the estimates are based.

3. In considering use of the perpetuity with growth method, it needs to be recognised that few companies can expect to exceed the cost of capital for long periods of time. As a guideline caution needs to be exercised in adopting a high growth rate, and for purposes of realism assessment of the feasibility of key assumptions, like the sales growth rate against the market potential, should be undertaken over a limited time horizon. One alternative to the perpetuity with growth that we have found used in practice involves estimating a growth rate corresponding with expected economic (e.g. GNP) growth plus inflation in a second time period of say five years beyond the assumed planning period, followed by a third time period using a simple perpetuity assumption.

Figure 5.3: Phasing growth rates over time

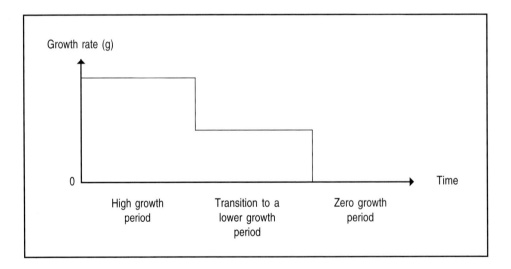

As mentioned earlier, in many cases the largest proportion of total value is generated from the continuing period. For this reason, many practitioners also look to other methods, but DCF methods have much to offer, because they can be interpreted and applied to support user judgement. In fact, they can be invaluable in terms of trying to understand the underlying issues involved in a valuation, although their acceptance in the market place for the specific case under consideration may be limited. For example, this is particularly the case for new issues where the use of Price Earnings (PE) multiples and the like have long been accepted practice.

Market relative valuation methods

Market relative valuation methods can be used in valuing the whole business and not just the TV. They are often used in Initial Public Offering (IPO) valuations, with the most popular method being the Price Earnings (PE) ratio. However, other methods like Enterprise Value: EBITDA, Price: Sales, and Market: Book are used, and will be reviewed in this section. Such methods are reckoned to give the most consistent results for steady, organically growing companies. For companies in periods of change and restructuring, these techniques have several shortcomings.

All of these methods seek to determine the value of a business by making a comparison between the financial characteristics of similar peer group companies, for which there is also a stock market valuation, and the company to be valued. The basic premise is that the relationship between the market value and some measure of financial performance for a number of peer group companies represents an appropriate basis for inferring the market value of the company to be valued.

Peer group comparators

A poorly selected peer group will make any relative valuation tenuous and great care needs to be exercised to ensure that companies for inclusion are realistic from an investor's perspective. Even if a satisfactory peer group has been selected, care should be taken not to exaggerate the effects of supply and demand on the underlying share price of some of the peer groups constituents particularly the less liquid ones. Further, one has to ask how to use the peer group data that is collected. For example, in terms of a PE relative valuation should the average ratio, the highest or the lowest be used? For example, at the time of writing, the UK food sector had around 22 companies with published PEs [†]. The historic sector PE was 17.43, the highest PE was 64.6 and the lowest PE was 7.3. This may be yet further complicated by the need to take account of the level of premium generally expected for acquiring control of a company.

As regards TV estimates using relative valuation methods there is one further major problem. The multiple(s) required are those for five years, 10 years or even longer and not today. Predicting such multiples is a minefield! Reflection upon the Asian crisis paints a simple but vivid picture of this. Plunging share prices have been reflected in substantially deflated PE ratios. Predicting what these will look like in five years time is anyone's guess!

Asset value analysis

In addition to DCF and Market Relative Valuation Methods, analysts commonly look at the realisable value of the underlying assets as well. Asset valuation analysis (AVA) methods measure the economic value of assets as if they are

---

[†]   Financial Times, October 31st, 1997 p.47.

sold. Such methods are a reasonable approach for companies that deal predominantly in assets that are relatively easily valued, like property companies. However, they represent a real problem for companies dealing with intangible assets, for example, drugs companies involved with patents, trademarks and brands.

If the collective use of assets within the business conveys a benefit greater than the sum of the individual assets, then realisable values will be irrelevant because they will always be lower than the economic value. However, calculating realisable values is useful for many reasons. It is useful at least to check that any realisable value is not greater than the economic value. A second reason is the inherent uncertainty of economic values. The advantage of considering realisable values is that it gives some indication of the extent of the loss if expectations about the earnings of the firm are disappointed. However, the relative importance of realisable values depends upon the control the shareholder has over the firm. Shareholders will only be in a position to enforce the sale of the firm's assets or their redeployment if they are planning to own a controlling interest in the firm.

Realisable values are not easy to calculate in practice because of the information typically available in the published financial statements is expressed in terms of historic cost, sometimes adjusted upwards following a revaluation. Furthermore, such a valuation only reveals the values of individual assets and not what value might result from them being grouped together.

Asset value analysis is often considered to be most suitable for:

- Asset–rich companies, especially after prolonged asset appreciation.

- Situations where cash flows are unpredictable or negative.

- Situations where asset revaluation has not been conducted for many years.

- Turnaround situations.

- Break–up situations (unbundling).

The cost of capital

The cost of capital is the weighted average financing rate on the blend of capital that a company employs to finance its activities. It is commonly known as the Weighted Average Cost of Capital or WACC for short.

The cost of capital used in a valuation can have a significant impact upon shareholder value, particularly where a perpetuity calculation is used to determine the residual value component. For example, in the analysis of the *Glaxo–Wellcome* acquisition by *James Capel*, a one percentage point increase in the group's cost of capital decreased the base case shareholder value per share by

75p [55]. However, it should not be overlooked that it is the benchmark against which value creation can be assessed.

Estimating the cost of capital

To estimate the cost of capital the steps to be followed are:

1. Estimate the cost of equity.

2. Estimate the cost of debt.

3. Work out the weighted average cost of capital.

Of these three steps the most difficult and controversial concerns the estimation of the cost of equity.

Cost of equity

There are a number of approaches available for calculating the cost of equity. Currently the most widely used is the Capital Asset Pricing Model.

Capital Asset Pricing Model (CAPM)

Modern financial theory suggests that the cost of equity can be estimated from analysing what return investors require when buying a share. The underlying premise of the CAPM approach is the more risk an investor is required to take on, the higher the rate of return that will be expected. CAPM relies on the assumption that every individual holding a risky security will demand a return in excess of the return they would receive from a risk–free security, to compensate for the extra risk taken on.

The CAPM cost of equity can be estimated using the following formula:

Cost of equity   =   Risk–free rate + (Beta x Equity risk premium)

For example, a company with a risk–free rate of 6%, a beta of 1.44, and an assumed equity risk premium of 4.5%, would have the following cost of equity:

Cost of equity   =   6%   +   (1.44 x 4.5%)   =   12.5%

Beta

The risk premium in CAPM is measured by the beta. This risk is called systematic, market, or non–diversifiable risk. This risk is caused by macroeconomic factors, like inflation, which affect the returns of all companies. If a company is affected by these macroeconomic factors in the same way as the market, then it will have a beta of 1, and will be expected to have returns equal to the market. Similarly, if a company's systematic risk is greater than the market, then the company will be priced such that it is expected to have returns greater than the market.

Perhaps it is easier to think of the beta as being a relative measure of volatility, the relative volatility being determined by comparing a share's returns to the market's returns. The greater the volatility, the more risky the share is said to be which relates directly into a higher beta. For example, if a share has a beta of 2.0, then on average for every 10% that the market index has returned above the risk–free rate, the share will have returned 20%. Conversely, for every 10% the market index has returned below the risk–free rate, the share will have returned 20% below.

Risk–free rate

The risk–free rate represents the most secure return that can be achieved. In theory the risk–free rate would be from a security with a beta equal to zero. In practice finding this security is empirically impossible. From a UK perspective, government bonds are largely insensitive to what happens in the share market and, therefore, have a beta of nearly zero, so can be used as an approximate to the risk–free rate. In most developed economies, government securities tend to be the best candidates for the risk–free rate, since the government in many countries guarantees payment.

There are generally three rates of government security: a current rate, long term (30 years) and medium term (10 years). In general the best rate is usually the medium term rate because:

● It is close to the length of the cash flow of the company being measured;

● It approximates to the duration of the stock market index portfolio;

● It is less sensitive to inflation, for example, and therefore has a smaller beta.

Equity risk premium

The equity risk premium represents the excess return above the risk–free rate that investors demand for holding risky securities. Until recently it seemed to be accepted practice to use an estimate of 8–9% for the risk premium of the equity market over the treasury bill rate. However in recent regulatory rulings in the UK much lower figures have been used (between 3% and 4½%) [56,57,58,59]. Furthermore, taking a forward looking view, much lower estimates can be derived. This is a very controversial issue that is the subject of a good deal of discussion and research.

Cost of debt

The cost of debt is the rate of return that debt–holders require to hold debt. To determine this rate the yield has to be calculated, this is often worked out by using discounted cash flow analysis, particularly the internal rate of return. The cost of debt should be calculated after tax as follows:

Cost of debt after tax = Cost of debt before tax x (100 − Marginal tax rate)

Weighted Average Cost of Capital (WACC)

The Weighted Average Cost of Capital (WACC) is calculated as follows:

$$\text{WACC} = \%\text{Debt}(K_d) + \%\text{Equity}(K_e)$$

Using the cost of equity and cost of debt figures calculated earlier the weighted average is calculated as shown in *Table 5.1*.

Table 5.1: Calculating the Weighted Average Cost of Capital (WACC)

	Cost	%	Weighted
Equity	12.500%	60%	7.5%
Debt	6.125%	40%	2.5%
WACC			10.0%

Cost of capital – a divisional business unit perspective

The approach outlined in this chapter enables a cost of capital for the whole company to be estimated, but it has some very real shortcomings. Often it is important to understand the value of the individual business units which, together, make up the whole company.

Companies can be thought of as consisting of a number of component businesses each of which has a different risk return relationship. However, the calculation of the divisional cost of capital is by no means a simple task. The cost of capital is, in fact, the weighted average of the costs of the separate sources of capital, in terms of equity and debt. In other words, when estimating the cost of capital for divisions of quoted companies, financial managers need to determine the cost of equity, the cost of debt and the capital structure for each of the divisions.

The main problem with the calculation of divisional discount rates is the availability of information. For publicly quoted companies finance theory provides an established existence of a relationship between risk and return. Risk is measured through the returns of a security, but the market data required does not exist for a non–traded firm or for a division of a publicly traded firm. However, there are two main approaches that can be used in such circumstances:

1. The analytical approach. [†]

2. The analogous approach.

[†]   Sometimes known as the 'cross–sectional' approach.

The analytical approach

Involves working from revenue, margins, asset saleability and other operating and structural characteristics. Data is developed from history or simulation and connected to market estimates of systematic risk and debt capacity via some linking mechanism. The analytical approach seeks to develop a relationship between accounting and market risk measures. If a stable relationship can be observed, divisional accounting data can be used to estimate the market risk of the division. However, although there is theoretical support for the analytical technique, there is no evidence that accounting and market linkages are stable. In other words, conflicting results from empirical studies illustrate that accounting returns fail to account for market risk.

The analogous approach

Involves finding firms that have market histories, as well as a restricted set of products very similar to the product line being examined. Analogous approaches differ from the analytical approach in that market data is utilised as a measure of risk. A series of analogous approaches have been developed, the most notable being the pure–play approach. This method is based on the premise that a proxy beta derived from a publicly traded firm, whose operations are as similar as possible to the division in question, is used as the measure of the division's systematic risk. The pure–play approach attempts to identify firms with publicly traded securities that are engaged solely in the same line of business as the division [60]. Once the pure–play firm is identified, its cost of equity capital is determined and then used as a proxy for the required divisional cost of equity capital. The presumption, of course, is that the systematic risk and capital structure of the pure–play are the same as those of the division.

Another analogous approach, the full–information approach, is based on the theoretical premise that a firm is simply a portfolio of projects; therefore the beta of a firm is the weighted average of its projects betas. This approach assumes that the beta of a division is the same, no matter which firm owns the division. The estimation of the cost of equity for a division is then a relatively simple process. Suppose a company has four business segments. The starting point would be to look for a number of quoted companies that have similar business segments in their portfolio and to calculate their equity betas. In addition, sales for each business segment are necessary to estimate the divisional betas, as these represent the weights for each business segment. Segment betas are then extrapolated by applying regression analysis assuming that the beta of a firm is the weighted average of its divisional betas.

The implication of analogous approaches varies in the degree of complexity, but the main strength of these techniques lies in the fact that market data is utilised as a measure of risk, thus validating their use in divisional cost of equity estimations.

Once cost of equity estimates have been undertaken for business units they can be fed into business unit cost of capital calculations. However, questions often arise about the appropriate debt : equity mix to use. In fact, careful consideration must be given to the question of the balance between the parent company's and the business unit's capital structure. A good case can be made for not basing the target capital structure for a business unit on the existing capital structure of the corporation as a whole, but on the debt capacity it could support as a stand–alone company. Corporate raiders have often taken advantage of management's failure to consider this fact.

One way of estimating stand–alone debt capacity and leverage is to ask: 'What would the business unit's target capital structure be after a leveraged buyout?' This requires a thorough analysis of its financial position, the degree to which its assets are specialised (and therefore of lower collateral value in the event of bankruptcy) and its industry and competitive position. Another way of determining a business unit's target capital structure is by comparing its present structure to that of its peer group companies and adjusting the structure according to its competitive position. This method assumes that the average company in a given peer group has reached its optimal capital structure, which may not be the case.

The cost of capital in practice

How the cost of capital is estimated in practice was investigated as part of a research study undertaken during 1995 [61]. The study was directed at the Finance Directors of the top 250 companies quoted on the London International Stock Exchange. Overall 142 companies (56.8%) responded. They consisted of 101(40.4%) companies which agreed to participate and 41 (16.4%) which refused for a variety of reasons.

All respondents undertook WACC calculations in one form or another. As regards estimating the cost of equity the use of a single method was exceptional and many respondents reported using more than one. In follow up interviews as many as four methods were reported as being used, though not with equal importance being attached to each. The method most used by responding companies was the CAPM and in follow–up interviews considerable importance was found to be attached to it. Other methods found to be in use were the dividend yield model, earning yield model, return on equity and *Gordon's* growth method.

As regards estimating the cost of debt, both market value and book value were found to be used in estimating yields. For estimates of the capital structure, the proportion of debt used in a WACC calculation was typically the result of a corporate policy on gearing, rather than a figure determined with reference to the debt capacity of individual divisions.

Most respondents were found to use a company–wide WACC, which supports the findings of a survey conducted in the US which showed that roughly one third of *Fortune 1,000* US companies used a single cost of capital [62]. In fact, only 21 companies in total responded that they used a divisional cost of capital.

Summary checklist

- Using the DCF approach to calculating the Terminal Value (TV) forces explicit consideration of the factors driving the value of a business beyond the planning period.

- In choosing which particular DCF formula to use it is important to consider what is driving value creation or destruction and for how long this situation is expected to last.

- Any DCF TV is highly dependent on the year selected to represent the cash flow to be valued. Often this is the last year of the planning period, but this may not be the most appropriate figure to use. For example, in cyclical businesses care would need to be exercised in understanding where the company is in the business cycle and the trend in the cycle.

- The cost of capital used can have a very significant impact on a DCF TV and hence its results should be crosschecked using other approaches to calculating the TV such as market relative valuation methods and asset value analysis.

- There are many market relative valuation approaches that can be used to estimate TV, all of which are reliant on being able to identify comparable peer group companies.

- It is wise to use as many 'reality' checks as possible to ensure that the characteristics of the situation being valued are consistent with the underlying basis of the TV calculation.

- WACC estimation can be thought of in terms of three steps – estimating the cost of equity, the cost of debt and the target debt to equity mix.

- The most difficult step is estimation of the cost of equity for which a number of different approaches can be used, but the most popular is the CAPM.

- Within a CAPM calculation there are many judgements that have to be made relating to the selection of the risk–free rate, beta and the equity risk premium.

- The objective in making a cost of capital estimate is to obtain a forward looking view. With this in mind, it is important to understand the distinction between the backward looking view of the cost of capital as calculated on the basis of past data and the forward looking view of the cost of capital calculated on the basis of forward looking data.

- The consideration of risk is essential in any discussion about what cost of capital to use. In simple terms, it is market related (systematic) risk that should be included in cost of capital estimates.

- The cost of capital can be calculated for business units as well as the corporation as a whole. This raises some additional complications because of the need to draw upon peer group company information for estimating betas and the like.

Chapter 6

Business Value, Economic Profit
and Performance Measurement

Chapter preview

- Calculation of Economic Profit approaches such as Economic Value Added (EVA®) and Strategic Value Added and how they can be linked to conventional measures of performance.

- Example of the use of Economic Profit as a performance measure and its linkage to calculating the value of a business.

- The distinction between the accounting perspective as expressed in traditional financial statements and the economic perspective as used in ascertaining value and value creation.

- Review of other performance metrics used to ascertain the value being created by a business.

Introduction

In previous chapters it has been shown how by using value drivers a free cash flow forecast can be estimated and the total value generated from such a free cash flow estimate for the planning period and beyond can be calculated. However, this is by no means the only way in which strategic value can be expressed or calculated. While the measurement of value is an essential starting point for developing a truly effective value–based management approach, it does not have to be calculated using free cash flow analysis. A number of alternative measures are available, of which economic profit is a good example. The advantage of using measures like economic profit is that they can be linked to performance measurement and executive compensation. However, do be aware that it is not the case that one must select either free cash flow or economic profit. There are a number of commercially available software valuation packages in the market that undertake the calculations for different measures.

While the different measures can be shown to produce the same result in principle, whether this is the case in practice will be dependent upon the assumptions made. Often differences do arise for many reasons we will explore later, not least of which is the purpose for which the measure is used.

Economic Profit, Economic Value Added (EVA®), and Strategic Value Added (SVA)

A valuation method called EVA® has been attracting much attention. It is one of a number that seek to analyse a business in terms of the economic profit earned in a given time period after deducting all expenses, including the opportunity cost of capital employed. In other words, a business is only 'truly' profitable in an economic sense if it generates a return in excess of that required by its providers of funds, i.e. shareholders and debtholders. Economic profit is not a new idea. *Alfred Sloan*, the patriarch of the *General Motors Corporation* is reckoned to have adopted the principles of economic profit in the 1920s, and the *General Electric Co.* coined the term 'residual income' in the 1950s, which it used to assess the performance of its decentralised divisions [63].

Economic profit recognises that the one major cost that the conventional profit and loss account does not take into account is the cost of the capital used in generating profit. Consequently with economic profit, from the net operating profit after tax (NOPAT) a capital charge is deducted based on the product of the capital invested in the business and the cost of capital.

Economic Profit = NOPAT – (Invested Capital x Cost of Capital)

For example, given a NOPAT of £1m, Invested Capital of £10 m and a cost of capital of 5%, the Economic Profit = £1m – £500,000, i.e. £500,000. Alternatively, it can be expressed as Economic Profit = (NOPAT% - WACC%) x Invested Capital i.e. the spread approach, where NOPAT% = (NOPAT ÷ Opening Invested Capital x 100. As shown in *Figure 6.1* NOPAT is a cash flow figure.

Figure 6.1: NOPAT is a cash flow number

NOPAT is a cash flow number which represents the constant level of cash flow that is generated by the business after making only replacement investment (but NOT growth investment) to maintain the cash flow generating capability of the existing assets. This can be shown to be so using the example in *Table 3.3* in *Chapter 3*. Let's start with EBITDA as follows:

	Year 1
EBITDA	31.5
less Depreciation	–10.0
EBIT	21.5
add–back Depreciation	10.0
less Cash tax	–9.4
Operating Cash Flow after tax	22.1
less Replacement Investment (Depreciation used as a proxy)	–10.0
Maintenance Free Cash Flow after tax	12.1

NOPAT is calculated as EBITDA less depreciation less cash tax i.e. £31.5m – £10m – £9.4m = £12.1m. Thus the maintenance free cash flow after tax for year 1 is exactly the same figure as NOPAT for year 1. Of course, this is only so if replacement investment is the same as depreciation.

What can be the attraction of using economic profit type approaches? There are arguably many, but there is one that seems to be particularly noteworthy and which has not been given a great deal of attention. Many organisations have developed performance assessment approaches that relate the profit generated in a given time period to the asset base, or capital employed in generating it.

As illustrated in *Figure 6.2*, this Return on Assets approach can be developed as a framework for assessing company performance along a number of dimensions. Relatively poor performance in terms of the Return on Assets generated in a given time period can be viewed in terms of margins (Return on Sales) and asset utilisation (Sales Generation). This Return on Assets can also be linked to capital structure (Gearing) and the markets perception of performance (Price Earnings and Market–Book).

Figure 6.2: Hierarchy of ratios

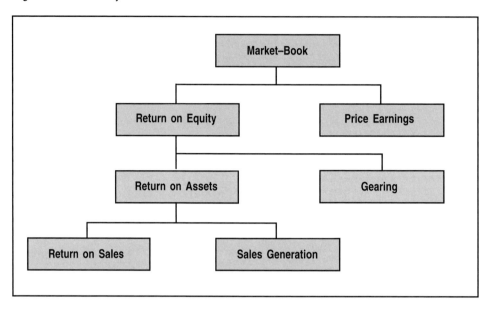

It can take a long time to implement performance assessment measures within companies, a point so often under estimated. As illustrated in *Figure 6.3*, the advantage of economic profit type approaches is that they can be linked to such conventional performance assessment frameworks.

Figure 6.3: Linkage between conventional financial ratios and economic profit approach

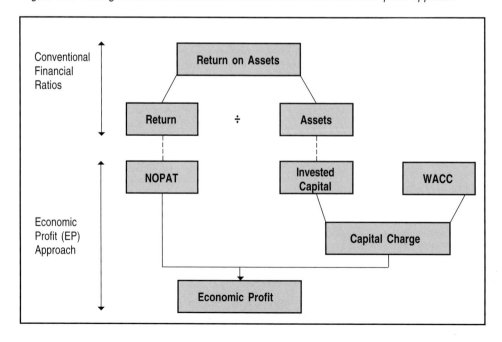

Linking economic profit and valuation calculations

As indicated, economic profit can be used to assess period by period performance and also for purposes of valuation. Economic profit is typically calculated over a specified time period, such as a year, with a positive economic profit figure signalling to management that value has been or will be created during the period in question, while a negative economic profit figure is indicative of value destruction. Economic profit (EP) can also be used for purposes of valuation as follows:

$$\text{Value} = \frac{\text{Invested}}{\text{Capital}} + \frac{EP_1}{(1+r)} + \frac{EP_2}{(1+r)^2} + \frac{EP_3}{(1+r)^3} + \dots\dots + \frac{EP_n}{(1+r)^n}$$

In simple terms, to link economic profit with value, the economic profit for each time period is estimated in the manner shown earlier, discounted at r (typically the weighted average cost of capital) and added to the Invested Capital. The actual mechanics of this calculation are illustrated in *Table 6.1*, which draws upon the data provided in *Table 3.1* from *Chapter 3*.

Please note that you will encounter economic profit 'branded' under many different headings. In the remainder of this book you will find it referred to as Strategic Value Added (SVA) to reflect the link between competitive advantage and the short– and long–term dynamics of value creation.

Table 6.1: Strategic Value Added calculation

Year	1	2	3	4	5	Beyond
	£m	£m	£m	£m	£m	£m
Opening Capital	125.0	128.0	131.2	134.6	138.0	141.6
IFCI	1.5	1.6	1.7	1.7	1.8	0.0
IWCI	1.5	1.6	1.7	1.7	1.8	0.0
Closing Capital	128.0	131.2	134.6	138.0	141.6	141.6
EBITDA	31.5	33.1	34.7	36.5	38.3	38.3
less Depreciation	10.0	10.0	10.0	10.0	10.0	10.0
less Cash Tax	9.4	9.9	10.4	10.9	11.5	11.5
NOPAT	12.1	13.2	14.3	15.6	16.8	16.8
NOPAT/Opening Capital %	9.7	10.3	10.9	11.6	12.2	11.9
Cost of Capital %	10.0	10.0	10.0	10.0	10.0	10.0
Performance Spread %	−0.3	0.3	0.9	1.6	2.2	1.9
Strategic Value Added (SVA)	−0.4	0.4	1.2	2.2	3.0	2.7

Cost of Capital %						10.0
Perpetuity						26.0
Discount Factor	0.909	0.826	0.751	0.683	0.621	0.621
Present Value of SVA	−0.4	0.3	0.9	1.5	1.9	16.1
MVA	20.3					
Opening Capital	125					
Business Value	145.3					
add Marketable Securities	0					
Corporate Value	145.3					
less Market Value of Debt	20					
Strategic Value	125.3					
Number of Shares (m)	100					
Strategic Value Per Share	£1.25					

In *Table 6.1* there is an initial negative SVA because of the negative performance spread, i.e. NOPAT/Opening Capital(%) is lower than the Cost of Capital (%). Thereafter, the SVAs are positive over the five–year period, resulting in a cumulative SVA over years 1 through to 5 of £4.2m. In the period 'Beyond', the SVA has been valued as a perpetuity providing a value of £16.1m (£12.7m ÷ 10% x 0.621), by far the largest contributor to total value. The sum total of these two values results in what is known as the Market Value Added, or MVA.

To use the SVA approach as a valuation method, the Opening Capital must be added to the MVA, the result representing the Business Value. In the absence of any marketable securities, this also represents the Corporate (Enterprise) Value. An estimate of the Strategic Value of the equity is found by deducting the market value of debt. If the resulting £125.3m of Strategic Value is divided by the 100m ordinary shares in issue, the result is a value per share of £1.25.

The economic versus the accounting perspective

There is an important difference between the economic profit perspective and the traditional accounting perspective portrayed in financial statements that needs to be considered at this point. The traditional accounting perspective can be traced back to the 1300's and focuses on stewardship reporting [64]. It explains to investors what has been done with their money and is principally backward looking. In particular, it assesses how much of the wealth created by the business has been realised in the form of tangible assets. It can be viewed as being a static model, concerned with the allocation of costs and revenues between relatively short time frames that draws upon accounting concepts. By comparison, economic profit type measures are more often concerned with the future economic profits that are likely to be generated over the life of a business and the risk associated with them.

The importance of the economic perspective becomes very clear within the context of ensuring that the opportunity cost of capital is achieved, that is what return would have been achieved on their investment in their next best use. Investors of all kinds require that at least their opportunity cost of capital is returned and this cannot be known unless economic returns are related to some notion of economic value. The need for such adjustments can be seen by looking at the market value versus the book value of companies listed on the stock market. For example, research in 1996 carried out by the Securities and Exchange Commission in the USA revealed that most companies going through mergers and acquisitions in the US during the period 1981–1993 were valued at between 2–9 times their book value [65]. As expected, software, communications and pharmaceutical companies were particularly highly valued, while banks, utilities and car companies were valued at the lower end of the range. Differences between the two groupings were attributable to their respective growth prospects at this time.

The SVA calculations that have been undertaken for the example company were based upon the accounting perspective. However, it is possible to move from the accounting to an economic perspective by making adjustments to the accounting statements to produce estimates of the economic returns and the economic capital associated with their generation. *Figure 6.4* illustrates the linkages between the two views of the value of a business. The underlying economic transactions of a business, that is, in cash flow terms are converted into accounting terms through the application of Generally Accepted Accounting Principles (GAAP).

Figure 6.4: The linkages between the accounting and economic perspective

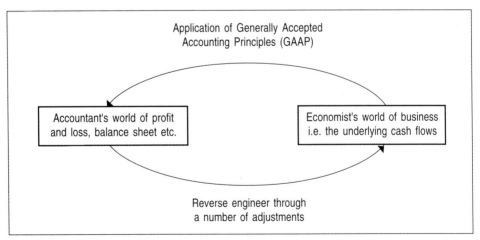

There are numerous potential adjustments that can, in principle, be made to convert accounting statements into their underlying economic form [66]. These adjustments are often referred to as value based adjustments. In practice, a handful of adjustments may be sufficient and some of the more noteworthy adjustments are shown in the *Figure 6.5* and an illustration of their impact in practice is shown in *Figure 6.6* with reference to *SmithKline Beecham*.

Figure 6.5: Adjustments from an accounting to an economic perspective

Goodwill	Cumulative value of previously written off goodwill is added back to the assets and depreciated.
R&D expense	Capitalised as a long term asset and depreciated.
Cumulative unusual losses/gains after tax	Treated as an asset to be written off over the future periods that are expected to benefit.
Operating leases	The present value of non capitalised operating leases are added back to fixed assets and depreciated.

Figure 6.6: Adjustments to Smithkline Beecham's financial results

SmithKline Beecham

SmithKline showed £1,791m of equity capital in its balance sheet at the end of 1997. However, in its accounts an amount of £1,535m of goodwill is shown that had been written off against equity reserves in the past. Additionally, the accounts show £695m worth of provisions that have been set aside. Making adjustments to the equity increases *SmithKline's* equity to £4,021m, but this takes no account of the fact that the company spends very large sums on research and development. For example, in 1997, it spent some £841m on research and development, all of which was written off against profits. What such write–offs ignore is that research and development is about creating products and profits for the future. As such, there is a good case for adding such expenditure to the balance sheet and treating it as part of the asset base against which a return should be generated.

To be more specific about the effect of such value based adjustments, let us consider the effect in our example of a land revaluation. The advantage of considering such an adjustment is that it will impact only upon the balance sheet and not the profit and loss account. This is because land is not depreciated, only any property built on it. For the sake of simplicity, we will assume there is no such property. The impact of such a revaluation upon SVA is illustrated in *Table 6.2*.

Table 6.2: Calculation of SVA assuming a land revaluation

Year	1	2	3	4	5	Beyond
	£m	£m	£m	£m	£m	£m
Original Opening Capital	125					
Add: Land revaluation	25					
Opening Capital	150.0	153.0	156.2	159.6	163.0	166.6
IFCI	1.5	1.6	1.7	1.7	1.8	0.0
IWCI	1.5	1.6	1.7	1.7	1.8	0.0
Closing Capital	153.0	156.2	159.6	163.0	166.6	166.6
EBITDA	31.5	33.1	34.7	36.5	38.3	38.3
less Depreciation	10.0	10.0	10.0	10.0	10.0	10.0
less Cash Tax	9.4	9.9	10.4	10.9	11.5	11.5
NOPAT	12.1	13.2	14.3	15.6	16.8	16.8
NOPAT/Opening Capital (%)	8.1	8.6	9.2	9.8	10.3	10.1
Cost of Capital %	10.0	10.0	10.0	10.0	10.0	10.0
Performance Spread %	−1.9	−1.4	-0.8	-0.2	0.3	0.1
Strategic Value Added (SVA)	−2.9	−2.1	−1.2	−0.3	0.5	0.2
Cost of Capital %						10.0
Perpetuity						1.0
Discount Factor	0.909	0.826	0.751	0.683	0.621	0.621
Present Value of SVA	−2.7	−1.7	−0.9	−0.2	0.3	0.6
MVA	−4.7					
Opening Capital	150.0					
Business Value	145.3					
add Marketable Securities	0					
Corporate Value	145.3					
less Market Value of Debt	20.0					
Strategic Value	125.3					
Number of Shares (m)	100					
Strategic Value Per Share	£1.25					

The effect of a £25m land revaluation is to increase the capital invested. Given that the profit does not increase, this results in a lower NOPAT/Opening Capital (%). The cost of capital remains unchanged because, as indicated in *Chapter 5,* it is calculated with reference to market values and not the information provided in the financial statements. The net result is a negative performance spread in Years 1 through 4 and very modest spreads thereafter. When the SVAs are calculated and accumulated, the result is a negative MVA of £4.7m. How then can the same Strategic Value per share result? The answer is that the higher initial capital value is added. However, let us stand back and reflect upon the implications of this. Despite the changing profile of the SVAs, the value of the business remains unchanged. This has important implications for managing the business, in that the original profile of SVA numbers could prompt management to take one set of actions that would be diametrically opposite to those actions taken under the revised profile of SVA numbers. Apparent management performance differs under the two scenarios and, it can be seen that in terms of providing a signal about the economic performance of the business, the figure for Invested Capital plays a significant role.

From a business valuation perspective, the value of a business appears to be independent of the opening amount of Invested Capital. This statement has to be accompanied by a word of caution in that the components that make up the value of the business are very different. For example, as *Table 6.3* shows, while the total value is the same for both the base case and the adjusted base case, its composition is very different. Again, the signals for potential management action as a result of these differing components could be interpreted very differently.

Table 6.3: Comparison of valuation components

	Base case		Base case adjusted for revaluation	
	£'m	%	£'m	%
Opening Invested Capital	125	86	150	103
Value of SVA for Years 1-5	4.2	3	−5.3	−4
Value of SVA beyond Year 5	16.1	11	0.6	1
Total	**145.3**	100	**145.3**	100

Applying Strategic Value Added in Practice – Hongkong and Shanghai Hotels Limited

The case of the *Hongkong and Shanghai Hotels Group* exemplifies the use of SVA. To recap on *Chapter 2*, The *Hongkong and Shanghai Hotels Limited* (the "Company" or "HK&S") is a listed company, but is closely held by its Directors and seven (7) major shareholders who hold approximately 50% of outstanding shares.

Initially limited to properties in Hongkong, it diversified and embarked on an oversees expansion program, and now has interests in projects in the United States, Australia, Indonesia, Thailand, the People's Republic of China, the Philippines and Vietnam. Its principal business comprises the ownership and management of prestigious hotel, commercial and residential properties in key destinations in Asia, Australia and the USA; its hotel management arm is The *Peninsula Group*. The currency crisis in the latter half of 1997 had a major impact upon The Company, with the company's share price falling to HK$5.50 at end of 1998.

As indicated in *Chapter 2*, the company's reported financial position at that time was as shown in *Table 6.4*.

Table 6.4: *Summary financial data for Hongkong and Shanghai Hotels Limited 1994 to 1998*

Balance Sheet as at December	1998	1997	1996	1995	1994
HK$ millions					
Net Assets	16,981	24,108	25,887	20,262	19,629
Shareholders' Equity	10,267	18,166	21,671	16,416	16,053
Ordinary Shares	578	581	586	539	539
Revaluation Reserves	8,210	14,211	16,762	13,189	13,155
Net Debt	6,689	5,406	3,873	3,597	3,398
Other data	**1998**	**1997**	**1996**	**1995**	**1994**
HK$ millions					
Sales	2,140	2,779	2,674	2,318	1,785
Share Price at period end [HK$]	5.50	6.40	14.6	11.2	8.95
Market Capitalisation at BS date	6,364	7,441	17,100	12,084	9,657
Number of Shares at BS date (millions)	1,157	1,163	1,171	1,079	1,079

As indicated in *Chapter 2*, at the point in time under review, the value of the business in 1998 looked at in terms of the market value of the equity, outside equity and other balances and net debt totalled HK$13,053 million, while net assets were HK$16,981 million. This corresponds with a negative Market Value Added (MVA) and indicates that the business is destroying value.

The equity (strategic) value of the business of HK$6.38 per share in free cash flow terms is summarised in *Table 6.5*.

Table 6.5: Strategic Value of Hongkong and Shanghai Hotels Limited

Period	Free Cash Flow HK $millions	Present Value Factor	Present Value of Free Cash Flow HK $millions
1999	746,976	0.9117	681,055
2000	915,424	0.8313	760,980
2001	1,110,824	0.7579	841,922
2002	1,337,488	0.6910	924,255
2003	1,600,418	0.6301	1,008,349
Beyond	14,280,777	0.6301	8,997,658
Business Value			13,214,220
Net Debt			–6,689,000
Other Balances			–162,000
Strategic Value			6,363,220
Number of Shares (m)			1,157,000
Strategic Value Per Share ($HK)			5.50

As demonstrated earlier, this strategic value can also be calculated using the Strategic Value Added (SVA) approach as illustrated in *Table 6.6*.

Table 6.6: Strategic Value Added of Hongkong and Shanghai Hotels Limited

Period	Economic Return on Capital %	WACC %	Spread %	Capital Invested HK$ millions	SVA HK$ millions	Present Value Factor	Present Value of SVA HK$ millions
1999	3.69	9.68	−5.99	16,981,000	−1,017,137	0.9117	−927,375
2000	4.60	9.68	−5.08	16,860,520	−856,305	0.8313	−711,835
2001	5.67	9.68	−4.01	16,720,763	−669,738	0.7579	−507,612
2002	6.94	9.68	−2.74	16,558,645	−453,322	0.6910	−313,263
2003	8.44	9.68	−1.22	16,370,589	−202,278	0.6301	−127,446
Beyond	8.56	9.68	−1.12	16,152,443	−1,871,666	0.6301	−1,179,250
MVA							−3,766,780
Opening Capital							16,981,000
Business Value							13,214,220
Net Debt							−6,689,000
Other Balances							−162,000
Strategic Value							6,363,220
Number of Shares (m)							1,157,000
Strategic Value Per Share ($HK)							5.50

This SVA analysis demonstrates how the Group is destroying value by generating an economic return on capital lower than the cost of capital. As indicated earlier in this Chapter , we need to ask whether the capital base is a realistic reflection of the economic capital invested. As indicated in the summary of financial performance in *Table 6.4*, the company has made substantial property revaluations. If you will recall from earlier, the effect of a revaluation upwards was to reduce the performance spread and SVAs, while the value of the business remained the same. In this case the effect of revaluation downwards has been to decrease and, therefore, improve a negative MVA.

Key value drivers were identified for the Group as being prices, investment in plant, property and equipment (PPE) and volumes (occupancy). Of these, there are clear problems with raising prices and volumes in a depressed Asian environment, although there might be scope elsewhere. However, PPE rationalisation could be seen as providing some potential for improving the negative performance spread. Other action that might be contemplated is considered in the next chapter.

Other performance measures

The importance of Invested Capital must be well understood in interpreting SVA type calculations. As we have illustrated, the profile of SVA numbers can vary substantially without the overall strategic value changing. The implications of this can be profound and could be political dynamite, particularly in a situation where the allocation of capital between business units is required. SVA results might evoke quite the opposite reaction to that intended if there is a lack of belief or acceptance in the Invested Capital upon which they are based.

Recently there has been some criticism of SVA type measures on the basis that they discourage growth. The argument goes as follows. Except for the rare cases where an investment has an immediate payback, growth oriented managers' take a short–term SVA hit. In other words, it encourages managers to milk the business as they quickly learn that the easiest way to improve SVA, at least in the short term, is by reducing and depreciating assets faster than earnings decline [67]. Pursued long enough, say three to five years, this creates a trap. Lack of investment can leave managers with such a depreciated asset base that any new investment will have a huge negative impact on SVA. With this being so, the long–term result of adopting SVA can be one of delivering enhanced returns but not long–term growth in the capital base.

SVA is not the end of the story as far as measuring performance is concerned. Other alternatives do exist in the form of Cash Value Added (CVA) and Total Shareholder Return (TSR) /Total Business Return (TBR). These metrics can be split into two groups; those that are used by investors looking from outside who want to evaluate the performance of their investment in the company and those that are used by the companies themselves to evaluate their performance (see *Figure 6.5*).

Figure 6.5: Users of the new metrics

User	Investor	Company Management
Metric	TSR, MVA	TBR, EVA, SVA, EP, CVA

CVA is the simpler approach in which SVA is adjusted to a cash and replacement–cost basis by adding depreciation and amortisation back to net operating profit, and accumulated depreciation is added back to the capital base. By eliminating the worst of Economic Profit's anti–growth or reinvestment bias, CVA takes an important step, but may still remain inadequate because CVA still measures performance on the margin.

The alternative used by *Monsanto* (see *Figure 6.6*) is to evaluate performance in much the same way as investors look at a share or, executives size up a potential acquisition. This approach is called Total Shareholder Return (TSR) at the company level and Total Business Return (TBR) when extended to business unit level. By comparing the beginning value of a business with its ending value, plus free cash flow over the period, TBR effectively replicates total shareholder return inside a company at the level of the individual business unit – see *Figure 6.7*.

Figure 6.6: Performance metrics at Monsanto Inc.

'Our objective was to put in place a system of economic based metrics that correctly measures shareowner value and that drives decisions so that shareowner wealth is continually enhanced over time. We selected Economic Value Added (EVA®) as *Monsanto's* overall metric. The EVA® financial management system will be supported by Total Business Return/Cash flow Return on Investment (TBR/CFROI) at the planning level.

TBR/CFROI is an investor oriented tool that measures a company's return to its shareowners over a period of time. TBR/CFROI can be used effectively to better determine the performance expectations in our stock price. These expectations can then be translated into EVA® targets for the company and its business units.

The power of combining these two metrics is that management now has at its disposal the most sophisticated techniques available to understand investor expectations. We can set business targets for achieving or exceeding these expectations, and then translate these goals into actions.'

Source: *Monsanto Inc. – 1995 Annual Report*

Figure 6.7: TSR and TBR

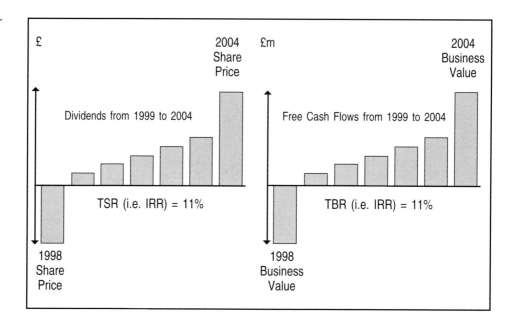

Summary checklist

- Economic profit measures like EVA® and SVA can be used in conjunction with the free cash flow approach to assess the performance of the business.

- Such measures of performance have the advantage of being capable of being linked with conventional financial ratio based performance measures.

- Caution has to be exercised in their measurement because of the impact of Invested Capital figure.

- Invested Capital typically needs to be adjusted to reflect economic reality by making value based adjustments. There is often a trade–off between accuracy and simplicity in choosing how many adjustments to make.

- New measures of assessing performance from a VBM perspective are evolving such as CVA, TBR and CFROI.

Chapter 7

Value Based Management Implementation

Chapter preview

- Λ framework involving a 10–step process that provides insight into understanding the potential to create value.

- A review of the Balanced Scorecard and Business Excellence Model.

- An overview of financial tools that can help in a VBM implementation.

- Key issues in implementing a Value Based Management system.

Introduction

In the preceding chapters, we have focused upon the measurement of value and the assessment of performance. Attention has been directed at many technical issues to ensure that as realistic a vision of value is obtained. In this, and the following chapter we consider the issues associated with implementing Value Based Management, (VBM) assuming that the necessary measurement of value and prospective performance assessment has been undertaken. It is also important to recognise that a focus on value creation can benefit all stakeholders not just shareholders. Questioning whether the focus should be on shareholders or stakeholders is the wrong question. The right question is how can value be created so that all stakeholders benefit over the lifetime of the organisation

10–Step Approach

Implementation does not happen by itself. It is one thing to measure prospective value, but quite another to achieve it. Companies implementing VBM have adopted two approaches, however, before we proceed to review these two approaches it is important to identify the overall framework of which these two can be seen to be a part. This framework was introduced in *Chapter 2* and can be viewed in terms of the following steps:

1. What is the managerial interpretation of your current value in the market?

2. What is influencing it, i.e. what are the key value drivers?

3. What are the apparent managerial actions for improvement and what are their impacts?

4. In light of 3., what should be the new vision?

5. What is the value of the new vision?

6. How does the vision translate into customer, shareholder and other relevant perspectives for the organisation?

7. How does the organisational vision look in terms of divisions/business units?

8. What is the divisional value?

9. What are the key divisional value drivers?

10. What do these divisional value drivers look like in terms of the micro drivers [†] and key performance indicators (KPIs)?

[†] Micro drivers: often referred to as the operational value drivers which are the business unit specific drivers such as sales volume, product mix, productivity etc.

In terms of *Hongkong and Shanghai Hotels*, we have looked behind the first five steps. We have considered how the HK$5.50 might be viewed from a managerial perspective, the key value drivers and the apparent managerial actions for improvement. The most immediate area for managerial action was the reduction of the asset base, for which improvements will produce a higher return and in turn a higher value [†]. For example, as illustrated in *Table 7.1*, an 8% decrease in fixed assets was found to increase the share price by HK$ 1. The business is still making a negative MVA, but with such a reduction in fixed assets it has improved.

Table 7.1: Strategic Value Added of Hongkong and Shanghai Hotels Limited

Period	Economic Return on Capital %	WACC %	Spread %	Capital Invested HK$ millions	SVA HK$ millions	Present Value Factor	Present Value of SVA HK$ millions
1999	3.69	9.68	−5.99	16,981,000	−1,017,137	0.9117	−927,375
2000	4.97	9.68	−4.71	15,597,240	−734,028	0.8313	−610,188
2001	6.14	9.68	−5.54	15,457,483	−547,462	0.7579	−414,936
2002	7.51	9.68	−2.17	15,295,365	−331,046	0.6910	−228,765
2003	9.15	9.68	−0.53	15,107,309	−80,002	0.6301	−50,406
Beyond	9.28	9.68	−0.40	14,889,163	−608,386	0.6301	−383,315
MVA							−2,614,985
Opening Capital							16,981,000
Business Value							14,366,015
Net Debt							−6,689,000
Other Balances							−162,000
Strategic Value							7,515,015
Number of Shares (m)							1,157,000
Strategic Value Per Share (HK$)							6.50

[†] This assumes that the primary business is not viewed as being property development. If that was the case, then reducing the assets would not be viewed as a sound business judgement. This view would probably regard the disposal of assets to improve business performance as being unwise and would be more disposed to speculating on an improvement in the property market.

Other sensitive areas for the business as reflected in the valuation model were prices, volumes, variable costs and the cost of capital. However, the opportunity for improving them in the short term given the current economic climate has to be seen as limited. Longer term improvements cannot be ruled out and if we assume that a 10% increase in prices could be achieved over the 5 year planning period, the estimated MVA becomes positive at HK$66,477,000 and the share price reflecting this would be HK$8.87.

These steps can be visualised as shown in *Figure 7.1*:

Figure 7.1

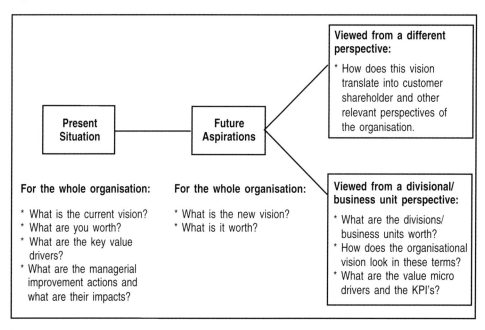

The key challenge is to understand and articulate the value inherent in a new future for the business. Put another way, what should be its future business model in terms of how it:

● selects its customers;

● defines and differentiates its offerings;

● defines the activities it will perform itself and those it will outsource;

● configures its resources;

● goes to market;

● creates value for customers; and

● captures profit.

Business models are changing all the time, particularly in response to changing circumstances. One has only to look at how new business models for retailing have emerged (e.g. retailing via the post/phone using catalogues) and are emerging (e.g. via the Internet). In order to respond, managers need to focus on the external environment, and to continually scan for the signals that things are changing. As an aid it is helpful to have the following questions in mind: Where in my industry is profit currently being made and by whom? How is that changing or likely to change? What is driving that change? What can my organisation do about it?'

Underneath these questions lies a more fundamental inquiry – 'What is the changing pattern of what customers need, want and are willing to pay for, and what business models respond most effectively to this changing pattern?' Every business model has a limited value creation life–cycle. Managers must act to create the next viable business model before they are overtaken by more responsive and innovative competitors. This is where the use of scenarios introduced in *Chapter 2* can be a very useful tool for helping to answer these questions and to address the remaining implementation steps outlined earlier, i.e.

- What is the value of the new vision?

- How does the vision translate into customer, shareholder and other relevant perspectives for the organisation?

- How does the organisational vision look in terms of divisions/business units?

- What is the divisional value?

- What are the key divisional value drivers?

- What do these divisional value drivers look like in terms of the micro drivers and key performance indicators (KPIs)?

Balanced Scorecard

There has been increasing concern in many organisations about the way that performance is currently measured. The development of global markets accompanied by intense competition, have necessitated a drive for quality and a search for continuous cost–improvement. Accompanying this drive has been the questioning of whether established methods of measurement and analysis are still wholly appropriate.

In all areas of business it has become clear that the needs of both customers and shareholders have to be satisfied, and that an emphasis upon one to the exclusion of the other will not be accepted. The challenge to meet these needs in a turbulent business environment means that businesses have to be able to respond to customer requirements with their internal delivery mechanisms, and also be able to update and change them as necessary. The implications of this are profound. To be successful, companies will need a broad set of performance indicators and not just a set focusing upon financial indicators of performance. What is more these indicators will have to be appropriate and relevant. To take a personal health example, the benefits of prevention via diagnosis are well known. What we require is an understanding of those things that really matter to our future well being. Dwelling upon the past or what has happened is only relevant insofar as it helps us make future decisions.

The Balanced Scorecard was developed to broaden the scope of performance indicators away from a preoccupation with financial performance [68]. This approach includes some financial measures, which are complemented by operational measures like customer satisfaction, internal process measurement and the organisational innovations and improvement to activities. All the latter require operational measures of strategy and represent the drivers of future financial performance.

As illustrated in *Figure 7.2*, the balanced scorecard allows managers to look at the business from four important perspectives:

● How do customers see us? (customer perspective)

● What must we excel at? (internal perspective)

● Can we continue to improve and create value? (innovation and learning perspective)

● How do we look to our shareholders? (financial perspective)

Figure 7.2: The balanced scorecard

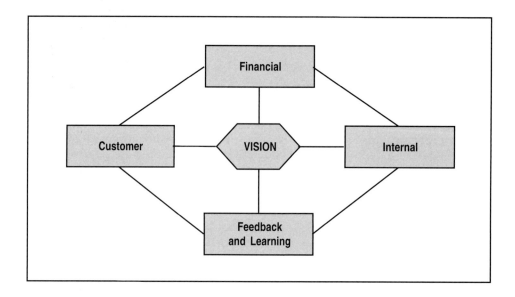

Each perspective considers important performance related issues in their own right. The customer perspective is seen as being particularly important. Meeting customer requirements has clear implications for the organisation's delivery mechanisms and the internal business perspective focuses upon the processes and actions that need to be undertaken within the organisation. The measures in the form of the resulting performance indicators will stem from the analysis of those features, which will have an impact upon customer satisfaction.

The innovation and learning perspective focuses on the dynamics of change. The contemporary business environment recognises that targets have to keep changing and need to be redefined: e.g. continuous improvements to products and processes are of necessity. As a result this perspective focuses on such challenges and measures them in terms of innovation, improvements and learning.

Last, but by no means least, is the financial perspective, which relates to shareholders. Key indicators are typically adopted which cover profitability, liquidity and increasingly, value creation.

While valuation models of the type discussed in the preceding chapters are invaluable for understanding the sources of value and the potential action required to improve it, there has to be a means by which this action can be translated into specific managerial action to make it happen. In this respect, the Balanced Scorecard can be invaluable for linking the vision with the managerial action essential to bring about improvement.

One of the key benefits of adopting a Balanced Scorecard approach is that it offers the potential to align business goals throughout the whole organisation. In other words the scorecard can be a vehicle for translating higher level business goals into a level of specificity appropriate for each level in the organisation and in doing so makes them actionable. The mechanisms for making this happen are the organisations key management processes, i.e. business planning, budgeting, performance reporting and incentivisation. Embedding the scorecard into these business processes ensures that alignment of goals is achieved throughout the organisation. See *Figure 7.3.*

Figure 7.3 Driving VBM down the organisation via the key management processes

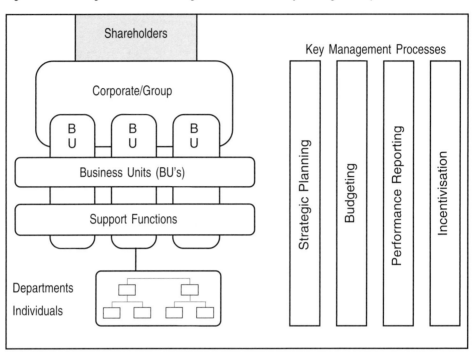

When used in this way the balanced scorecard becomes part of a businesses value based management system for understanding the dynamics of value creation. See *Figure 7.4*.

Figure 7.4: Value Based Management system

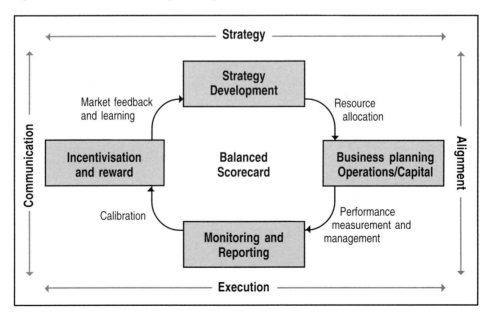

In *Figure 7.4*, there are four key processes to a typical value based management system, which are part of a self–reinforcing circle:

1. Strategy development. This is concerned with articulating the organisations vision and expressing it in terms of the specific strategic goals that need to be achieved from the shareholder, customer, employee and innovation perspective. Here the scorecard has a role as the mechanism for translating a vision into more tangible goals. In essence its about deciding what should an organisation do and culminates in the allocation of resources to do it.

2. Business planning is about how the strategy should be specifically carried out. In other words, what specific actions, activities and programmes need to be undertaken in order to achieve the organisation strategic gaols. The role of the scorecard is to ensure that the execution is in alignment with the strategy.

3. Monitoring and reporting is about measuring the organisation's performance in executing its strategy. Put another way, it answers the question: how well did the organisation do what it said it would do. Here again the scorecard has a role as the measurement framework for making this assessment.

4. The incentivisation and reward stage concerns rewarding people for the attainment of the strategic goals and in so doing the role the scorecard performs here, is that of a mechanism for communicating how successful or not the organisation was. Additionally, the scorecard functions as a tool for capturing the key lessons that the business has learned or must learn to achieve its vision.

British Telecommunications plc (BT) introduced the Balanced Scorecard in 1994 to help strengthen the connection between its corporate strategy and operational activities [69]. The need for a connecting mechanism was identified during project Break–out, a group wide improvement and process re–engineering drive that involved more than 1000 teams between 1993 and 1994. As part of project *Break–out BT* focused on the strategy and planning process, and although there was a high understanding of, and commitment to, strategic objectives, there was some concern as to how effectively these were being linked to operational activities. So the strategy and planning team identified the scorecard as a powerful tool for making strategic objectives come alive in operational terms.

Focusing upon a handful of measures that are the most critical components of the desired objectives is a feature of the approach. As a result of this, its implementation by organisations has been shown to have two major benefits:

1. It brings together in a single management report, many of the disparate elements of a company's competitive agenda.

2. It helps to prevent decisions being made that are not in the interests of the whole organisation, even though it may benefit one particular part of the business. By forcing senior managers to consider all–important operational measures together, the balanced scorecard lets them see whether improvement in one area may be achieved only at the expense of another.

Business Excellence Model

Many organisations that have adopted or are adopting the principles of value we have discussed in connection with Strategic Value Analysis have emphasised the achievement of business excellence, focusing more upon the Business Excellence Model than the Balanced Scorecard.

Figure 7.5: The Business Excellence model

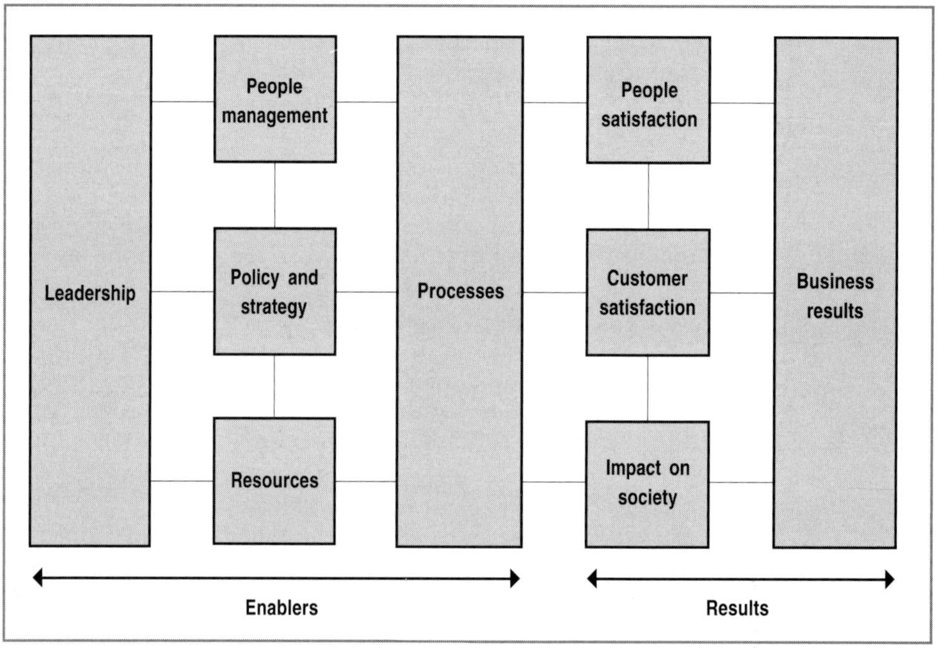

A standard European model has been developed which is used to measure an organisations 'level' of excellence. This business excellence' model is based on the principle that in order for an organisation or team to succeed, there are a number of key 'enablers' on which it should concentrate its efforts, and it should measure its success through a number of key 'results' areas.

The key enablers by which organisations judge themselves are:

● How well the organisation is led.

● How well its people are managed.

● How far its policy and strategy are developed and implemented by its leaders and people.

● How well it manages its resources and develops and manages its processes.

The key result areas by which the model then measures successes are those identified with reference to the balanced scorecard:

- How far its satisfies its customers.

- How well motivated and committed its workforce is.

- How the local and national community outside the organisation views its activities in terms of its contribution to society.

- Its key business results – profit, return on capital employed, shareholder earnings, achieving budgets.

Business excellence and ICL Plc [70]

ICL has used the Business Excellence Model as part of its business value implementation initiative. *ICL* has its roots in a company originally incorporated in 1915. It is an unquoted European–based information technology company, which supplies hardware, applications software and services of all types, operating in over 70 countries worldwide. Its headquarters are in Slough.

In the early 1990s *ICL*, in order to focus on its customers, decentralised its organisation into specific vertical markets and horizontal businesses. *ICL* needed to understand better its competitive advantages. Therefore *ICL* developed a management methodology to enable its business managers to understand the components of its competitive advantage and how this translates into increasing shareholder value.

The business value programme began in April 1994. It was designed by *Professor Roger W. Mills* and *Mr. I. Neill*, Director of Strategic Planning in ICL and centred on the seven value drivers which underpin shareholder value creation. As has been illustrated, these drivers emphasise the link between strategy and finance and in particular they focus on the key determinants of competitive advantage. They are often expressed in terms relevant to the organisational culture, which for *ICL* are: understanding the market, understanding the customers' needs, understanding the competition and understanding *ICL's* distinctive capabilities.

Figure 7.6: Value Drivers at ICL

Value Driver		Key Drivers
● Planning Horizon	Strategy	– capability -- customer -- competitors -- market
● Revenue Growth	Revenue	-- forecasting -- portfolio analysis
● Operating Profit ⎤ ● Cash Taxes ⎦	Profit	-- value chain -- tax management
● Fixed Asset Expenditure ⎤ ● Working Capital Movement ⎦	Balance Sheet	-- asset management
● Cost of Capital	Cash	

The *ICL* developed a Management Model, (see Figu*re 7.8)* which was introduced in September 1997. *ICL's* vision, mission and objectives became underpinned by strategies and programmes that sought to answer two fundamental questions, namely, in which businesses do we invest our resources and how does the parent influence and relate to the businesses under its control. The programmes that underpinned the business strategies were founded on the business excellence model, and lead to a set of milestones (strategic agreements) which are reviewed three times a year (business reviews).

A key feature of the model is the extent to which it recognises that implementation of any business value initiative must focus upon all of the stakeholders and not just the shareholder. Indeed, this is a key feature of the Business Excellence Model.

Figure 7.7 ICL Management Model

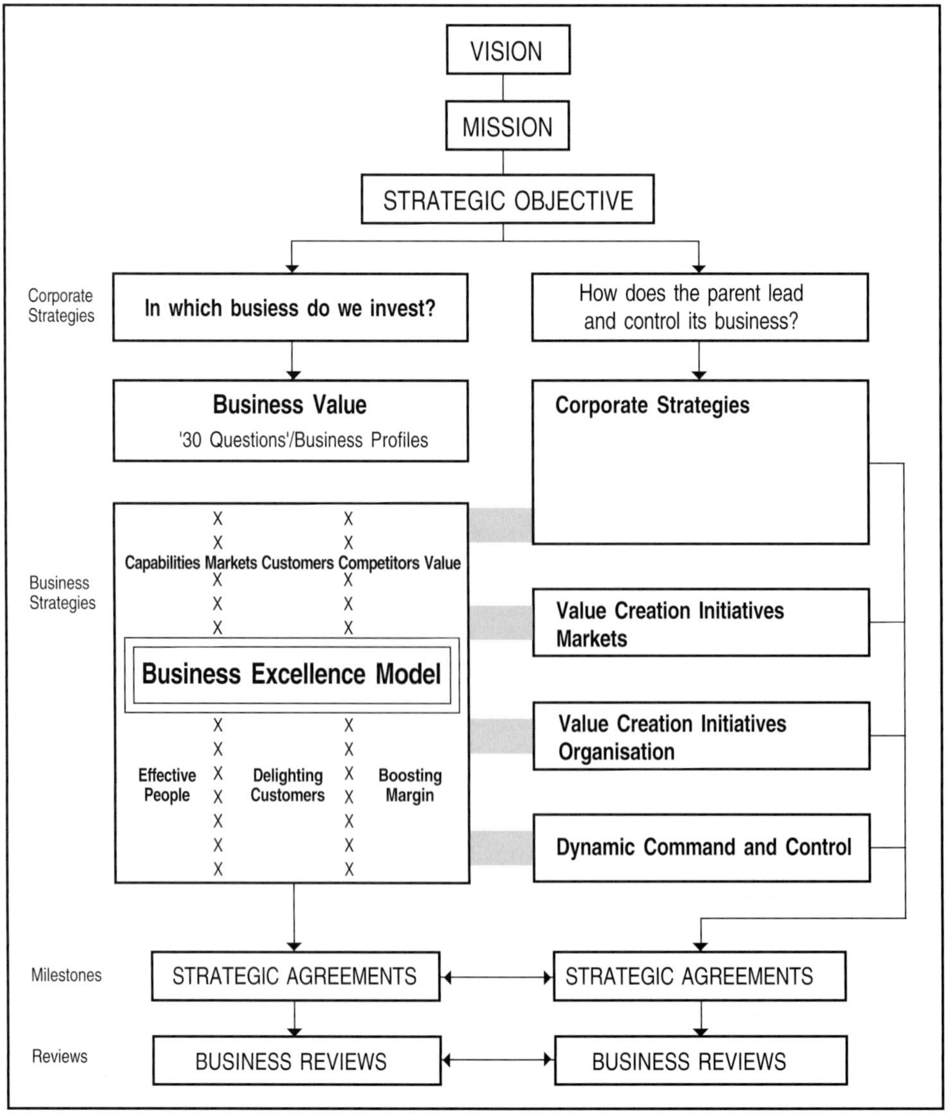

10–Step Approach Revisited

While the specific implementation approach adopted by businesses may differ, we have found that the 10 steps outlined earlier and reproduced below capture the sequence of events that need to be followed. The first five challenge the current vision, value and potential for improvement for the whole business. However, in terms of implementing any changes that are identified as being warranted, approaches like the Balanced Scorecard and Business Excellence Model are invaluable, but they need to be related to a vision that has been clearly articulated and which can be related specifically to financial performance. Such approaches can not only be applied at the overall business level, but also within business units/divisions. In fact, it would be difficult to imagine successful implementation without driving change down through the business as a whole. The advantage of the 10 step approach outlined is that it relates the use of such approaches to fundamental questions about value and performance in financial terms at the overall business and business unit levels.

10–Step Approach

1. What is the managerial interpretation of your current value in the market?

2. What is influencing it, i.e. what are the key value drivers?

3. What are the apparent managerial actions for improvement and what are their impacts?

4. In light of 3., what should be the new vision?

5. What is the value of the new vision?

6. How does the vision translate into customer, shareholder and other relevant perspectives for the organisation?

7. How does the organisational vision look in terms of divisions/business units?

8. What is the divisional value?

9. What are the key divisional value drivers?

10. What do these divisional value drivers look like in terms of the micro drivers and key performance indicators (KPIs)?

Financial tools to support implementation initiatives

A key feature of the approach is the need to be able to measure value. This becomes increasingly difficult the further down the business that implementation proceeds and for which some financial tools can be invaluable. One area that is always particularly contentious is the separation of costs. For example, the measurement of Strategic Value Added can be undertaken for the overall business and for each of the business units or divisions it comprises. While some costs may be separable and distinct for each of the business units or divisions, others, like those relating to information technology, may be joint or shared. There is clearly a need to be able to identify and analyse such costs for which Activity Based Costing is invaluable. In addition, there are occasions when the cost base itself needs to be challenged, for which Target Costing can be helpful.

Activity Based Costing (ABC)

Traditional costing takes the standpoint that products consume costs directly whereas ABC takes the view that it is the products that consume activities and then it is the activities that consume costs. Put another way, ABC assumes that activities cause costs to be incurred and that products or customers consume activities in varying amounts. A link is made between activities and products/services by assigning the cost of activities to products based on an individual product's demand for each activity. A typical ABC system involves:

1. The identification of the key activities that take place in the organisation.

2. The creation of a cost centre for each major activity.

3. The assignment of costs to activity cost pools.

4. The determination of the cost driver for each activity cost pool.

5. The determination of the unit cost for each activity.

6. The assignment of the costs of activities to selected cost objects (for example, products) according to the cost object's demand for each activity.

Stage 1 requires that activity analysis is undertaken in order to identify the major activities performed in the enterprise. Activities are simply the tasks that people or machines perform in order to provide a product or service. For example, in retail banking this would correspond with processing a deposit, issuing a credit card, processing a cheque, setting up a loan, opening an account or processing monthly statements, and so on. In a support activity like a personnel department, activities would be recruitment, remuneration, training, union negotiation, personnel administration, staff welfare, and so on.

Stage 2 requires that a cost centre be created for each activity.

Stage 3 requires that costs are analysed and assigned to the appropriate activity cost centre. For example, the total cost of processing a deposit in a retail bank might constitute one activity cost centre for all deposit processing related costs, with separate cost centres being created for each type of deposit account if different types of deposits consume resources differently. In a personnel department, recruitment may constitute an activity cost centre including recruitment related costs like advertising, interviewing, contracts, and induction.

Stage 4 is concerned with the identification of the factors that influence the cost of a particular activity. The term 'cost driver' is used to describe the events or forces that are the significant determinants of the cost of the activities. For example, if the number of deposits processed generates the cost of processing deposits, then the number of deposits processed would represent the cost driver for deposit processing activities. In the case of a personnel department the cost drivers could be advertising, interviewing, contracts, and induction.

The cost driver selected for each cost centre should be the one that, as closely as possible, mirrors the consumption of the activities represented by the cost centre. Examples of cost drivers that might be appropriate for other retail banking activities include the number of:

- applications processed for setting up a loan;

- statements mailed for processing monthly statements;

- mortgage payments past due date for processing activities relating to mortgage arrears.

The next stage divides the cost traced to each activity cost centre by the total number of driver units in order to calculate a cost per unit of activity.

Finally, the cost of specific activities is traced to products or services or customers or channels (referred to as cost objects) according to their demand for the activities by multiplying unit activity costs by the quantity of each activity that a product consumes.

The total cost of a product or service is then found by adding the individual costs of the activities that are required to deliver the product or service. In other words, a product or service can be viewed as a bundle of activities. ABC focuses on the costing of these activities and the bundling of them into products, customers or any other cost objects.

ABC seeks to measure as accurately as possible those resources consumed by products or services, whereas traditional costing systems typically just allocate costs to products or services. Unlike a traditional costing system, the ABC approach offers considerable advantages. The traditional approach might allocate deposit transaction processing costs to customers, or different types of deposit accounts, on the basis of the number of customer accounts which could lead to distorted product costs if deposit processing costs are driven by the number of transactions processed. Allocating cost according to the number of customers will lead to low value deposit accounts that involve numerous 'over–the–counter' transactions being under–costed, whereas high value long–term savings accounts requiring very few transactions will be over–costed. In contrast, an ABC system would establish a separate cost centre for deposit processing activities, ascertain what causes the costs (that is, determine the appropriate cost driver, such as the number of transactions processed) and assign costs to products on the basis of a product's demand for the activity.

Two main benefits of ABC are improved cost accuracy and cost control:

Cost accuracy:

● Improved product/service strategy.

● Improved pricing strategy.

● Greater understanding of the product line profitability.

● Reflection of all overhead costs (e.g. administrative) associated with the product.

Cost control:

● More accurate appreciation of what drives costs.

● Changed emphasis towards managing costs as a result of a better appreciation of cost causation.

● Recognition of time consuming/inefficient operations.

It is often with regard to cost management and cost control that ABC can deliver greatest benefit. Traditionally, the control of non–variable costs is problematic and ABC is advantageous because it concentrates attention upon managing the business on the basis of activities that make up the organisation. By collecting and reporting the costs consumed by the significant activities of a business, it is possible to understand and manage costs (including non–variable costs) more effectively. It cannot be stressed enough that the focus of attention within ABC is to control business costs by directing attention towards the activities that drive them. In other words, the aim is to manage the activities rather than the costs. By managing the forces that cause the activities (that is, the cost drivers), cost will be managed.

In our experience managers are frequently surprised at how many activities are performed within their organisation that do not add value to any product or service but consume significant resources. These non–value added activities have often continued because they have been hidden by traditional cost systems. ABC makes them visible so that steps can be made to eliminate them. Furthermore, by merely knowing the costs of activities potential 'non–value added' activities are highlighted so that steps can be taken to improve profitability. Consider a situation where loans staff in a retail bank, as a result of costing activities, are informed that it costs £100 to process and maintain loans of less than £500. They become aware that it is questionable to provide loans of less than £500 unless more cost effective ways can be found of undertaking this activity. Similarly, if the cost of processing and maintaining low value and high value mortgages is the same, management is made aware that it is more profitable to focus on high value rather than low value mortgages.

In fact, an ABC–based SVA (Strategic Value Added) of a product or service can be estimated using [71]:

Revenue – (ABC Cost + Capital Employed x Cost of Capital)

This extension to ABC looks very simple and requires that the capital employed (often referred to as Invested Capital) for each product (or other cost object) be determined and that a risk–adjusted rate for that capital be identified. The practicalities are more difficult, but there is little doubt that there are benefits to be obtained in linking SVA with ABC, as can be demonstrated with reference to the following example. Product 1 sells for £100, has an ABC cost of £30, but requires capital employed of £100. Product 2 also sells for £100 and has an ABC cost of £30, but it requires capital employed of £1,000. If the cost of capital is 10%, then the first product has a positive SVA of £60 (£100 – £30 – £100 x 10%), whereas the second has a negative SVA of £30 (£100 – £30 – £1,000 x 10%). While Product 1 creates wealth, Product 2 destroys it, both have the same £70 ABC profit.

Integrating ABC and SVA focuses attention upon the economic return of products, customers, and channels, as well as rewarding the more efficient use of capital. That is not to say that there are no practical problems. The allocation of capital is fraught with all sorts of problems, as is the estimation of the cost of capital at business unit level, let alone product level. For this reason when ABC and SVA are integrated, the concept of dedicated– and non–dedicated capital has to be taken into consideration. Dedicated capital is that which can be traced meaningfully to cost objects while non–dedicated capital cannot. By contrast, non–dedicated capital is employed to support the facility or the enterprise, but it is not directly associated with the manufacture of products or the servicing of customers and channels. A good example of such capital is the short–term investment and cash that firms accumulate to acquire other firms.

This approach could be applied in the decision about how to use or allocate capital employed. At the product and customer level, there are three ways in which capital can be employed more efficiently. First, the assets can be used to support a different product or customer mix. For example, if a machine is used to produce an equal volume of the two products described above, it will generate an SVA of £30 (£60–£30) for every pair of products that it produces. If the mix can be changed so that it is 100% of the first product, then the SVA for a pair of products climbs to £120 (£60 X 2). Second, dedicated assets that are no longer required can be sold and the capital used for new investment purposes that have a higher SVA. Third, additional assets that are required to support the new product or customer mix can be acquired.

Target Costing

Target costing is a comprehensive approach designed to reduce costs which begins even before there are any plans for new products and it involves the examination of *all possible* ideas for cost reduction at the product planning, research and development, and the prototyping phases of production. Furthermore, it is held out to be not just a cost reduction technique, but part of a comprehensive strategic profit management system.

Target costing involves the following steps:

1. Determine a target market price based on marketing factors, at a level that will permit a company to achieve its desired market share and volume.

2. Desired profit is then deducted from the market price to determine the maximum allowable, or target, product cost.

3. This target cost which is not the actual cost then forms the basis for making product decisions.

Target costing works backwards from a target competitive price to a target cost, at a specified demand level, which then becomes the goal to achieve. This target cost then needs to be evaluated in the light of required inputs. In other words, the "top down" target cost is compared with a "bottom up" view, the latter possibly being determined using ABC.

As indicated, target cost is simply the difference between estimated sales price and target profit, i.e.

Target Cost (TC) = Estimated Sales Price – Target Profit.

Estimating sales price is viewed as being the starting point in determining the target cost which involves considering for each product:

● Characteristics of anticipated consumers/target market.

● Product life cycle.

● Desired/potential sales volumes.

● Competitors' strategies.

To estimate selling price, TC begins with the collection of market information. To ensure such information is fully used, an organisational link must be established closely between the market research department and others involved in the development process. The flow of information must not be limited to one direction. Market research is needed to ensure the market orientation of the whole development process. It has to explore customers needs, wishes and expectations, transform these into specific requirements of product function. Specific requirements are weighted according to their degree of importance to the customer and a distinction is made between hard (need to fulfil purpose) and soft (convenience and personal value) functions.

Whilst estimating sales price is the starting point, there is the key question of who decides the price first? For price followers price taking may well be the normal practice. But, there is another approach known as 'pricing by functions'. The fundamental belief of the approach is that a product price can be decomposed into thousands of elements, each of which reflects the value. For example, in pricing automobiles by functions the following factors would be among those to be considered:

● Style.

● Comfort.

- Operability.

- Reliability.

- Quality.

- Attractiveness.

The total of the costs associated with each function gives an estimate of the sales price.

Once the sales price and the target profit have been estimated the target cost can be estimated from the difference of the two. This represents the cost from the customers' perspective, after taking due consideration of the return required by the company. In very simple terms, this can be thought of as representing 'the voice of the customer' and may be very different from the cost that would be determined using conventional cost accounting practices of the type described in earlier sections. The challenge is making the two equal one another which can be achieved by one or more of the following:

- reviewing existing costing practices to see if they provide an accurate picture of the real cost – i.e. by use of activity analysis;

- purchasing components more cheaply without sacrificing quality;

- reducing the number of components;

- redesigning components to achieve economies.

In practice, target costing comprises two processes, which involve:

1. planning a specific product that satisfies customers' needs. Then establishing the target cost from the target profit and sales price of this new product, and

2. realising the target cost by using value engineering and a comparison of target costs with achieved costs.

A key part of the target costing process relates to value engineering and variety reduction.

Value engineering is an interdisciplinary, team–orientated approach for generating ideas and converting them into constructive improvements for a key component so as to achieve a lower cost or greater benefit. It is required at early stages of the product development process to ensure that target costs are attained. This is because almost all elements of product costs are *fixed* by the time the drawings are complete. However, unlike other cost reduction tools value engineering aims to maintain and desirably improve quality levels whilst reducing cost.

Summary checklist

- A focus on value creation can benefit all stakeholder not just shareholders. Questioning whether the focus should be on shareholders or stakeholders is the wrong question. The right question is how can value be created so that all stakeholders benefit over lifetime of the organisation.

- At the heart of creating value, irrespective of how each stakeholders defines it, is the issue of what is the organisations business model that enables it to not only create but extract value from its environment. Not only do managers need to understand the current business model but also watch for the signals that it might need changing.

- The Balanced Scorecard and Business Excellence Model are powerful frameworks for understanding value creation from different perspectives and for implementing a Value Based Management approach.

- Activity Based Costing (ABC) and Target Costing are two tools that can be used in support of the implementation of a VBM programme

- The crux of Value Based Management is that of making disciplined decisions in line with value creation principles and can be seen in terms of a 10 step approach directed at:

  - the execution of a robust strategy;

  - that creates value for all stakeholders;

  - by making disciplined decisions;

  - through the organisations business processes;

  - by focusing on the key underlying drivers of value;

  - and ensuring alignment of value creation throughout the organisation;

  - that is consistent with a common behaviour and culture.

Chapter 8

Implementing VBM – The Evidence

Chapter preview

- Review of recent research into the implementation of shareholder value.

- Key implementation issues facing organisations implementing VBM.

- Observations on the evidence of successful implementation.

- Enablers to successful implementation.

Introduction

Having reviewed and discussed differing approaches and key issues in the process of understanding VBM and its implementation, this concluding chapter provides evidence from some recent research into the implementation of shareholder value in large international companies. Summary findings related to those factors found to be key in successful implementation, their implications and some observations, on the benefits to be derived and the pitaflls to be avoided, are presented. The study undertaken was an in–depth analysis over a number of years in three large international companies. The findings are recognised as not necessarily gereralisable. We recognise the need for further research: this is part of our future agenda.

Key features of successful implementation

Recent research into the implementation of shareholder value in large international companies found the following key features of successful implementation:

- Value creation is viewed as a key objective and not as another management initiative.

- Top management commitment to the shareholder value approach is essential, building on the research and understanding of the ideas underpinning the approach.

- The process needs to be championed at CEO/director level, with delegation for implementation.

- The importance of communicating the ideas and concepts of the discounted cash–flow based, rather than accounting, view of future performance to the senior management of the business(es) involved is essential.

- A process of developing awareness is vital, followed by a more formal education process for the business unit/company heads, led by corporate centre, related to developing an understanding of the application of the concept within the company.

- The process of strategic planning is critical in implementing the approach. The preparation of realistic strategic reviews by business units, with alternative strategies evaluated using shareholder value concepts are a primary planning tool. These are an important key to success in maximising shareholder value and considerable effort is needed to establish an effective way of managing and enabling this. Of particular significance is the role of the corporate centre in challenging and coordinating this process.

- The development of the value–based framework and management processes needs to be supported by the strategic planning process, and managed by the corporate centre. Although the value–based approach may be adopted for strategic purposes, it is typically very difficult to integrate it into all the financial reporting systems. A step–by–step approach is often favoured, adopting the approach initially where the greatest benefit can be realised. It is important to recognise that to fully align the value–based approach and financial reporting requirements will take considerable effort.

● The commitment of management to the process is critical for success and reward systems could play an important part in principle, but care needs to be exercised in the timing of the introduction of such schemes.

Key implementation issues

Companies intending to implement value based management need to be aware of a number of key issues identified in companies that have been involved in implementation:

Timescale/Speed

The process of implementation usually takes longer than anticipated. There needs to be a preparedness, and planning, to overcome resistance to the changed requirements, particularly implementing to manage the ongoing business, and making the measures meaningful at operational level. Companies determining to manage for shareholder value are committing themselves to a lengthy, and costly, process. Conversely, speed in being able to create value is seen as crucial, and an inability to hasten the process and enable speedy decisions can be frustrating. Management processes will need to be improved, and the use of external consultants can be a motivating force to speed up the process of change.

The Role of the Champion/Change Leader

Successful move to the shareholder value approach needs a driving force – someone who wants shareholder value to be the way the company is measured and who is prepared to take the lead. Recognition of the lengthy timescale of implementation and the need for a driver/leader of that change involves a considerable resource requirement to provide an effective leader of the change, who may be 'tied up' as a key resource for a number of years. During this time they will need to work and develop their own strategy and style to be effective in their role of *influencing* and *enabling* management in the implementation. Managements must be aware of and plan for such a considerable resource, and plan to ensure continuity and succession in this key role.

Role of the Corporate Centre

Leaders of the change are often part of the corporate centre, and the centre becomes a primary resource, in terms of education and training in the application of the concepts, providing support, guidance, feedback to *enable and influence* management and to coordinate and *challenge* management. The need for a good linkage between those teams working in the centre, who are usually competent and knowledgeable about value–based concepts, who are familiar with the corporate language, and those who are out in the business units, in operational positions – at the customer face is essential. Research has identified that the role of the centre in influencing the progression of the implementation, in manner and scope, has been identified as an important factor. There has been a need to 'gather in' the business units to communicate, educate and train in the new concepts by which they will be measured, which has strengthened the *influencing* role of the centre. If the role of the centre (parent) is critical to the implementation then also is an understanding of *how* the centre (parent) has achieved the outcome – i.e. how it has itself added value is an important element, and what has it had to spend so much time and effort doing to achieve the outcome. In multibusiness companies, the corporate parent may be considered central to corporate strategy and decision making. *Goold, Campbell and Alexander* [73] state:

> *'The parent is at the heart of corporate strategy decisions.... Our research has highlighted the significance of the parent's influence on decisions much more than its basic cost...'*

In their research on successful parenting they identify the 'essence' as:

> *'creating a fit between the way the parent operates – the parent's characteristics – and the improvement opportunities that the parent addresses'*

If accepted as the key corporate objective, the implementation of shareholder value techniques to create value in a business is a 'parenting opportunity'. One of the potential areas of parenting opportunity identified by *Goold, Campbell and Alexander* (1994), that of "the need for specialist expertise not possessed by the business" certainly fits the requirement for the implementation of the shareholder value concept at corporate level. The cascading of this expertise and the ability of the corporate centre to achieve this is seen as a significant issue and is closely linked to the parenting role and consideration of the value they add to the process.

Level of cascading throughout the company

Once the underlying concept has been 'bought into' by the top management, the next step is the transference/cascading of the concept in the development of value–creating strategies and value–creating processes undertaken with the business unit/operating company heads. Research has found that heads of the business units/operating companies had been involved fairly early in the process but the further transference into the management of the business units/ operating companies had not generally progressed very far, which was a reflection of the difficulty identified of making the approach meaningful at operational level. There had been significant commitment to making the approach visible and to promoting understanding within the companies, but providing tangible means of measuring and managing value for those working with customers, clients or in operations had not progressed as far as the companies would have liked. This is recognised as an important issue: substantiated by a number of contributors on value–creation:

> *'need to drive value–based management throughout the company'*
>
> (McTaggart, Kontes and Mankins) [74]

'need to focus on value drivers at the grass roots level'

(Copeland, Koller and Murrin) [75]

The fundamental principle behind value–based systems (whichever metric is adopted) is based on well–established and accepted finance theory, which has been suggested by a number of writers (*Rappaport* [76, 77]; *Stewart* [78]) as easy to understand. However true this may be at corporate level, this is only likely to be the case further down the company if the 'shareholder value talk' is in terms that make sense to an individual's work. The primary objective of a value–based system is to link the firm's strategies and management performance evaluation to the creation of shareholder value. Successful use of these approaches lies in their effective implementation throughout an organisation – and this means ensuring that those involved in transferring the concepts are able to portray them in practical ways rather than as a complicated theory. The requirements for implementing the process at corporate level are likely to be different from implementation at lower levels in the company, and companies must recognise that they needed to address such issues as resource implications for educating and training below business unit/operating company head level and the degree of cascading that would be necessary.

Previous research (*Mills et al* [79], *PA Consulting Group* [80], *Price Waterhouse* [81]) has shown that the principles underpinning shareholder value calculation are well established. They are found in use in project finance and in the evaluation of major investments; they are used to give insight into how the market values a business. They are used in decisions concerning restructuring, mergers and acquisitions which are seen as routes to value creation. These use of the techniques are very much the role at corporate level, where the need to understand which parts of the business deliver value, and which are using excessive amounts of capital without making sufficient returns is a vital part of the function of managing the portfolio. Although widely used at corporate level, research also shows that there are only a handful of companies who have progressed to the stage where a value based management approach is used *throughout* the company. The following is the comment of a divisional manager at one major European multinational (*Price Waterhouse* [81]):

> *'The CFO is really hooked on this shareholder value thing. Out here in operations where it counts, it means nothing. It simply hasn't been translated into terms that we relate to. We haven't got a clue how to put it into practice.'*

The evidence is that good progress has been made in adopting the shareholder value approach as an effective strategic planning tool, and that this has produced a higher standard of strategy development at corporate and business unit level in determining the markets and businesses in which to operate and investments that are necessary to support those decisions. This has been the primary focus of the companies and there are differing views as to the timescale and the level of cascading that will occur in the future. However the need to establish shareholder value measures that are usable at operational level is accepted as an important issue, along with the recognition that this will require skill and commitment to manage and overcome any resistance to change, to prepare management to learn and anchor new behaviour.

Cost of capital

Estimating and understanding the cost of capital is a fundamental issue in shareholder value, and an area which poses some difficulty when attempting to address the issue of the cost of capital is its estimation for each business unit/ operating company. Often a simplistic view is adopted, whereby the total company cost of capital is used and applied to each of the business units/ operating companies, but it is recognised that this is not an accurate policy and considerable work is being undertaken to assess and establish different costs of capital for individual business units/operating companies. This is an area that has typically been managed at corporate level and there is some concern about the level of understanding of the issue below that level, which would need addressing in terms of communication and education in the future. Without an adequate assessment and understanding of the cost of capital it is not possible to determine how much, or whether, value has been created or destroyed.

Change from established financial/management reporting systems

Moves to change the financial/management reporting systems to a discounted cash flow basis are essential. The degree of development has been limited, and often the current reporting systems are not adequate or always suitable for value reporting. This is an area where it is recognised that existing accounting systems which still form the basis of performance reporting need to be adapted to incorporate more fluidly operational value drivers to ensure that management and measurement are aligned operationally.

The ongoing nature of the approach

Maximising shareholder value is accepted as a key corporate objective by many companies; it is not viewed as another management initiative. The intention is that the company will be managed and governed to maximise value for its shareholders and stakeholders on a long term basis; the objective is to ensure that the company produces returns on its capital in excess of its cost of capital. There is a powerful sense that the process of implementation does not have a finite end; it requires continual review, feedback and the drive/momentum of top management to sustain the approach.

Observations on successful implementation of value–based management

To enable companies to achieve their objective of value creation, there appears to be a vital requirement for the company to be *directing* the value creation process. This is a requirement significantly greater than initial implementation. It requires accepting the long term responsibility for maintaining and retaining the processes and behaviours necessary to satisfy the key objective of achieving a return on capital greater than the cost of capital, and providing the *direction* to achieve it. For this, although initial championing is important, there is a need for the value direction process to become an integral, ongoing part of the management. Directing value to produce a return greater than the cost of capital influences the whole company and encompasses all functions of the company. An analogy could be drawn with the development of IT. Some years ago the role of IT was not recognised as spanning all functions and influencing the whole business in the way it is now accepted to do.

Value direction is not necessarily a finance led responsibility but a coordinating role, bringing a set of value direction skills, covering a number of functional areas and a set of prerequisites for the creation of value. The following list is not suggested as exhaustive but indicative of the types of skills necessary:

● developments of applied corporate finance;

● financial culture;

● cost of capital;

● change management;

● value performance measurement;

● strategic planning;

● value metrics;

● value budgets;

● value plans;

● education and training;

● investor relations;

● information management/technology;

● internal audit;

● executive compensation;

● recruitment/resourcing.

A number of these prerequisites cover the development of value reporting systems, an important area for the management and measurement of value. Many of the current accounting systems are developed for the requirements of statutory financial reporting, and internal management accounting and performance reporting systems are drawn from these. A development would be to separate the financial reporting requirement entirely from the internal reporting system to allow these to be developed exclusively for value reporting which would better reflect the requirements at different levels in the organisation. Although financial information is necessary at certain levels, physical measurements, e.g. in terms of customers satisfied, are more relevant and appropriate at operational level, where accrual accounting is usually unhelpful for management and measurement. Value direction means ensuring that the necessary links are in place between building budgets and targets in physical value terms and enabling their transfer to financial data at higher levels, to enable everyone to 'get on with managing the business in meaningful terms for creating value'.

What can VBM facilitate?

- Strategic and financial planning at corporate and business levels.

- Corporate investment decisions.

- Evaluation of revenue expenditure programmes.

- Corporate finance decisions with respect to dividend policy, investor relations, treasury management, and financial decisions.

- Performance targeting, measurement and reward systems.

The critical success factors found to enable the implementation of VBM include:

- Top management being visibly committed to, and actively interested in, VBM.

- Value to shareholders being set alongside ambitions to satisfy other corporate values and not being seen as the sole objective of the organisation.

- Inclusion of planning, control and reward systems.

- Education in the use of cash based financial tools and exposure to strategic analysis tools.

- Willingness to explore areas where value creation may be weak.

- Early hand–over of management of the process to management rather than be championed by external consultants.

- Having a clear plan early on for a roll–out programme throughout the organisation.

- Management of expectations so that managers will realise that the lags will occur between investing in change and reaping the rewards.

On the other hand, in implementing a VBM programme a number of don'ts include:

- Avoid degeneration into a number crunching exercise where modelling and measurement take a life of their own.

- Avoid falling into the trap of playing the 'VBM game' through manipulating terminal values of business strategies which need to be tested against external assumptions.

● Do not apply VBM only to a particular area of the management process or business e.g. capital investment decisions.

● Avoid being 'bullheaded'. It is sometimes tempting to accept compromise in order to make headway, e.g. defer changes in reward systems.

The key benefits to be derived from VBM include:

● Development of a common framework for integrating long range strategic plans, capital programmes, acquisitions, short term budgets, etc.

● Rewards systems that align behaviour and motivation.

● Realisation that a trade–off not only exists between large investment projects, but also between these and revenue programmes.

● Performance measurement has become much more outward focused and geared to achievements relative to competitors and also relative to market conditions.

Summary checklist

● The raison d'etre of VBM is the influence on behaviours throughout the organisation in line with value creation principles.

● Whilst the exact recipe for implementing VBM will vary from organisation to organisation there are a number of key issues that have been found to be important to addres; these include timescales, role of champion, role of corporate centre, level of cascading, cost of capital and changes to reporting systems.

● Successful implementation of a VBM programme in the long-term is dependent on having in place a 'Value Direction' process that provides the organisational direction to enable the tenets of VBM to become part of the ongoing management and culture of an organisation.

● The real benefits of a VBM programme are derived from viewing it as an organisational change process, not a one-off finance initiative.

● Several companies have already started on the value journey. The step is to identify where the company is in terms of the four stages identified in the chapter and, second, to understand what needs to be done to implement VBM.

References

1 Mills, R. W. and Print C., Strategic value analysis, shareholder value and economic value added - what's the difference?, *Management Accounting*, February 1995, p.35–37.

2 'Valuing companies – a star to sail by', *The Economist*, 2 August 1997, p.62.

3 Griffith, I., *Creative Accounting: How To Make Your Profits What You Want Them To Be*, Unwin Hyman, 1986.

4 Smith, T., *Accounting for Growth: Stripping the Camouflage from Company Accounts*, Century Business, 1992.

5 Pijper, T., *Creative Accounting: The Effectiveness of Financial Reporting in the UK*, MacMillan, 1994.

6 Jack, A., 'Accounting tricks 'fool City analysts'', *Financial Times*, December 8, 1993, p.24.

7 Terazono, E., 'JBA hit by world according to GAAP', *Financial Times*, 26 September 1997, p.20.

8 Valuing companies – a star to sail by, *The Economist*, 2 August 1997, p.62.

9 Simmonds, A. and Azieres O., *Accounting for Europe: success by 2,000 AD?*, Touche Ross, 1989.

10 Roberts, C.B., Salter, S. B. and Kantor,T.J., 'The IASC comparability project and current financial reporting reality: an empirical study of reporting in Europe', *British Accounting Review*, Vol.28, 1996, pp.1–22.

11 Nobes, C.W., 'Classification of Financial Reporting Practices', *Advances in International Accounting*, Vol.1, 1987, pp.1–2.

12 Doupnik,T. and Salter, S.B., 'An Empirical Test of a Judgmental International Classification of Financial Reporting Practices', *Journal of International Business Studies*, No. 1, 1993, pp.41–60.

13 Nobes, C., *International Guide to Interpreting Company Accounts 1996-1997*.

14 Beresford, D., 'US should import UK improvements', *Financial Times*.

15 Wright, P.D. and Keegan, D.P., 'One foot in the future', *Financial Times*, 24 April 1997.

16 Wright, P. D. and Keegan, D. P., *Pursuing Value: The Emerging Art of Reporting on the Future*, PW Papers, Price Waterhouse LLP, 1997.

17 Barron, M. and Lawless, J., 'Growth of no account', *Business Magazine*, September 1988.

Henry, D. and Smith, G., 'Letter to Financial Times', *Financial Times*, 27 June 1991.

18 Bowen, R. M., Burgstahler, D. and Daley, L. A., 'Evidence on the relationships between earnings and various measures of cash flow', *The Accounting Review*, Vol.LXI No.4, 1986, pp.713–725.

Gombola, M. J. and Ketz, J. E., 'A note on cash flow and classification patterns of financial ratios', *The Accounting Review*, Vol.LVIII, No.1, 1983, pp.105–115.

Rayburn, J., 'The association of operating cash flow and accruals with security returns', *Journal of Accounting Research*, Vol.24, 1986, Supplement, pp. 112–133.

Wilson, G. P., 'The relative information content of accruals and cash flows: combined evidence at the earnings announcement and annual report release date', *Journal of Accounting Research*, 1986, Vol.24, Supplement, pp. 165–200.

Wilson, G.P., 'The incremental information content of the accrual and funds components of earnings after controlling for earnings', *The Accounting Review*, Vol.LXII, No.2, 1987, pp.293–322.

Bowen, R.M., Burgstahler, D. and Daley, L. A., 'The incremental information content of accrual versus cash flows', *The Accounting Review*, Vol.LXII, No.4, 1987,pp.723–747.

Bernard, V. L. and Stober, T. L., 'The nature and amount of information in cash flow and accruals', *The Accounting Review*, Vol.LXIV, No.4, 1989, pp.624–652.

Charitou, A. G. and Ketz, E., 'An empirical examination of cash flow measures', *ABACUS*, Vol.27, No.1, 1991, pp.51–64.

Arnold, A. J., Clubb, C. D. B., Manson, S. and Wearing, R. T., 'The relationship between earnings, funds flows and cash flows: evidence for the UK', *Accounting and Business Research*, Vol.22, No.85, pp.13–19,1991.

Simmonds, A. and Azieres, O., *Accounting for Europe: success by 2001AD?*, Touche Ross, 1989.

Nobes, C. 'Accounting for differences in the Far East: are they inscrutable?', *Management Accounting*, October 1994, p.36.

Solomon, E., 'Return on investment: the relation of book yield to true yield,' in *Research in Accounting Measurement*, R. J. Jaedicke, Y. Ijiri, and O. Nielson, (Eds.) American Accounting Association, Chicago, 1966), pp.232–244.

19 Madani, H. H., 'An empirical examination of the explanatory power of accrual earnings versus cash flows: UK industrial sector', Ph.D.Thesis – Henley Management College/Brunel University, 1996.

20 Lukasik, T., 'What drives asia pacific valuations? evidence from the markets', *CPS Global Review*, Vol.111, No.VII, October 1997, p.5.

21 *Employment performance*, McKinsey Global Institute, November 1994.

22 Copeland, T.E., 'Why value value?', *The McKinsey Quarterly*, 1994, No.4, pp. 97–109.

23 Bughin, J. and Copeland, T. E., 'The virtuous cycle of shareholder value creation', *McKinsey Quarterly*, 1997 No.2, pp.157–167.

24 Kotter, J. P. and Heskett, J. L., *Corporate Culture and Performance*, The Free Press, New York, 1992.

25 Europe's New Capitalists, op. cit.

26 Europe's New Capitalists, *Fortune*, Feb 15, 1999, Vol.139, Iss.3, p.104(1).

27 Brewis, J., Corporate Germany starts to listen to its shareholders, *Corporate Finance*, February 1999, pp.18–23.

28 Sheridan, T., A new frame for financial management, *Management Accountin (UK)*, February 1994, p.26.

29 Cooper, R., *When Lean Enterprises Collide*, Boston: Harvard Business School Press, 1995, p.7.

30 Cooper, R., The changing practice of management accounting, *Management Accounting (UK)*, Vol.74, No.3, March 1996, pp.26–35.

31 Kaplan, R. S., New roles for management accountants, *Journal of Cost Management*, Fall 1995, p.13.

32 Albright, T. and Cooper R., *Brookwood Medical Center (A)*, Boston: Harvard Business School, 1996.

33 Abrahams, P., 'Relaunch into more enterprising culture', *Financial Times*, 29 July 1993, p.20.

34 Mills, R. W. and Weinstein, W. L., 'Calculating Shareholder Value in a Turbulent Environment', *Long Range Planning*, Vol.29, No.1, 1996, pp.76–83.

35 Ogilvy, J., *Probabilities: Help or Hindrance in Scenario Planning*, GBN Publication on Internet, June 1996.

36 Rappaport, A, 'CFOs and strategists: forging a common framework', *Harvard Business Review*, May–June, 1992.

37 Miller, M. and Modigliani, F., 'Dividend Policy, growth and the valuation of shares', *The Journal of Business*, October 1961.

38 Bennett-Stewart III, G., *The Quest for Value*, Harper Collins, New York 1991, pp. 289–298.

39 Miller, M. and Modigliani, F., 'Dividend policy, growth and the valuation of shares', *The Journal of Business*, October 1961.

40 Porter, M. E., *Competitive Strategy: Techniques for Analysing Industries and Competitors*, The Free Press, 1980.

41 Rumelt, R. P., 'How much does industry matter?', *Strategic Management Journal*, Vol., No.3, March 1991, pp.167-186.

42 Rumelt, R. P., 'How much does industry matter?', *Strategic Management Journal*, Vol., No.3, March 1991, pp.167-186.

43 Porter, M.E., *Competitive Advantage*, The Free Press, 1985.

44 Kay, J., *Foundations of Corporate Success: How Business Strategies add value*, Oxford University Press, 1993.

45 Prahalad, C. K. and Hamel, G., 'The core competence of the corporation', *Harvard Business Review*, Vol.68, No.3, May/June 1990, pp.79–93.

46 Aaker, D.A., 'Managing assets and skills; the key to a sustainable competitive advantage', *California Management Review*, Winter 1989.

47 Source, Aaker, op.cit.

48 Williams, J.R., 'A new way to understand business competition', Working Paper, Graduate school of Industrial Administration, Carnegie-Mellon University, May 1985

49 Ansoff, H. I., *Implanting Strategic Management*, Prentice Hall, New Jersey, 1984.

50 Slywotzky, A.J., *Value Migration*, Harvard Buisness School Press, 1996

51 Mills, R. W. et al.,'*The Use of Shareholder Value Analysis in Acquisition and Divestment Decisions*, Chartered Institute of Management Accountants, 1997.

52 Rappaport, A., *Creating Shareholder Value*, Free Press, New York, 1986, p.85.

53 Mauboussin, M. and Johnson, P., 'Competitive advantage period 'CAP': the neglected value driver', *Frontiers of Finance*, Credit Suisse First Boston, op.cit., p.9.

54 Mills, R.W. and Weinstein, W.L., 'Calculating shareholder value in a turbulent environment', *Long Range Planning*, Vol.29, No.1, 1996, pp.76–83.

55 James Capel Equity Research, *Pharmaceuticals: In search of Shareholder Value*, May 1995, p.19.

56 Blanchard, O.J., Movements in the equity premium, *Brookings Papers on Economic Activity,* Vol.2, 1993, pp.75–138.

Blanchard, O.J., The vanishing equity premium, Working Paper, MIT, October, 1992.

Jenkinson, T., The equity risk premium and the cost of capital debate in the UK regulated utilities, Working Paper, Keble College, Oxford, 1993.

Scott, M.F., 'The cost of capital and the risk premium on equities', *Applied Financial Economics 2*, 1992, pp.21–32.

Siegel, J.J., 'The equity premium: stock and bond returns since 1802', *Financial Analysts'* Journal, January-February, 1992, pp. 28–38.

57 Blanchard, O.J., *Movements in the Equity Premium, Brookings Papers on Economic Activity 2*, 1993, pp. 75–138.

Blanchard, O.J., The Vanishing Equity Premium, Working Paper, MIT, October, 1992.

Chan, K.C., Karolyi, A. and Stulz, R.M., 'Global Financial Markets and the Risk Premium on U.S. Equity', *Journal of Financial Economics*, Vol.32, 1992, pp.137–167.

Fama, E. F. and French, K., 'Business conditions and expected returns on stocks and bonds', *Journal of Financial Economics,* Vol.25, pp.23-49.

58 Jenkinson, T., 'The Equity Risk Premium and the Cost of Capital Debate in the UK Regulated Utilities', Working Paper, Keble College, Oxford, 1993.

Jenkinson, T., 'The cost of equity finance: conventional wisdom reconsidered', *Stock Exchange Quarterly*, Autumn 1993, pp.23–27.

59 Brown, S. J., Goetzmann, W.N. and Ross, S.A., 'Survival', *Journal of Finance* Vol.50, 1995, pp.853–873.

60 Fuller, R. and Kerr, H., 'Estimating the divisional cost of capital: an analysis of the pure play technique', *Journal of Finance*, December 1981, pp.997-1009.

61 Mills, R.W., et al., The Use of Shareholder Value Analysis in Acquisitions and Divestment Decisions by Large UK Companies, Chartered Institute of Management Accountants, 1997.

63 Gitman, L.J. and Mercurio, V.A., 'Cost of capital techniques used by major US firms: A survey and analysis of Fortune's 1000', *Financial Management*, Winter, 1982.

63 McConville, D. J., 'All about EVA', *Industry Week*, 13–14 April, 1994, pp.1–3.

64 Bernstein, P., *Against the Gods: The Remarkable Story of Risk*, Wiley, 1996.

65 Edvinsson, L., 'Developing intellectual capital at Skandia', *Long Range Planning*, Vol.30, No.3, June 1997, pp.366–373.

66 Up to 164 according to Stern Stewart - 'EVA Seminar', *Business Intelligence*, 16 February 1996, London.

67 Stalk, G., 'How EVA puts a chokehold on growth', *The Globe and Mail (Toronto)*, Friday, June 26,1998.

68 Kaplan, R.S. and Norton, D.P., 'The balance scorecard measures that drive performance', *Harvard Business Review*, January/February, 1992, pp.71–79.

    Kaplan, R.S. and Norton, D.P., Putting the balanced scorecard to work, *Harvard Business Review*, September/October, 1993, pp.134–137.

69 *Measuring Business Excellence* – Vol.1, No.1., 1997.

70 Courtsey of: Neill, I., Director of Strategic Planning, ICL and Stephanie Bell, Managing Director, The Bell Partnership, February 1998

71 Cooper, R. and Slagmulder, R., Integrating activity-based costing and economic value added, *Management Accounting*, New York, Jan 1999.

72 Print, C.F., Value Direction: The Implementation of Shareholder Value - The Way Forward, Henley Working Paper 9822, 1999.

73 Gould, M., Campbell, A. and Alexander, M., *Corporate Level Strategy: Creating Value in the Multibusiness Company*, John Wiley & Sons, 1994.

74 McTaggart, J.M., Kontes, P.W., and Mankins, M.C., *The Value Imperative: Managing for Superior Shareholder Returns*, The Free Press, 1994.

75 Copeland, T., Koller, T. and Murrin, J., *Valuation: Measuring and Managing the Value of Companies*, John Wiley & Sons, 1994.

76 Rappaport, A., *Creating Shareholder Value*, The Free Press, 1986.

77 Rappaport, A., *Creating Shareholder Value*, The Free Press, 1998.

78 Stewart, G.B., *The Quest for Value*, Harper Business, 1991.

79 Mills, R.W., et al., 'The use of shareholder value analysis in Acquisitions and Divestment decisions by large UK companies', Henley Management College, 1996.

80 P.A. Consulting Group, *Managing for Shareholder Value: Survey UK and Ireland*, 1997.

81 *CFO: Architect of the Corporation's Future, Price Waterhouse Financial and Cost Management Team*, John Wiley & Sons, 1997.

%	1	2	3	4	5	6	7	8	9	10
Period										
1	0.990	0.980	0.971	0.962	0.952	0.943	0.935	0.926	0.917	0.909
2	0.980	0.961	0.943	0.925	0.907	0.890	0.873	0.857	0.842	0.826
3	0.971	0.942	0.915	0.889	0.864	0.840	0.816	0.794	0.772	0.751
4	0.961	0.924	0.888	0.855	0.823	0.792	0.763	0.735	0.708	0.683
5	0.951	0.906	0.863	0.822	0.784	0.747	0.713	0.681	0.650	0.621
6	0.942	0.888	0.837	0.790	0.746	0.705	0.666	0.630	0.596	0.564
7	0.933	0.871	0.813	0.760	0.711	0.665	0.623	0.583	0.547	0.513
8	0.923	0.853	0.789	0.731	0.677	0.627	0.582	0.540	0.502	0.467
9	0.914	0.837	0.766	0.703	0.645	0.592	0.544	0.500	0.460	0.424
10	0.905	0.820	0.744	0.676	0.614	0.558	0.508	0.463	0.422	0.386
11	0.896	0.804	0.722	0.650	0.585	0.527	0.475	0.429	0.388	0.350
12	0.887	0.788	0.701	0.625	0.557	0.497	0.444	0.397	0.356	0.319
13	0.879	0.773	0.681	0.601	0.530	0.469	0.415	0.368	0.326	0.290
14	0.870	0.758	0.661	0.577	0.505	0.442	0.388	0.340	0.299	0.263
15	0.861	0.743	0.642	0.555	0.481	0.417	0.362	0.315	0.275	0.239
16	0.853	0.728	0.623	0.534	0.458	0.394	0.339	0.292	0.252	0.218
17	0.844	0.714	0.605	0.513	0.436	0.371	0.317	0.270	0.231	0.198
18	0.836	0.700	0.587	0.494	0.416	0.350	0.296	0.250	0.212	0.180
19	0.828	0.686	0.570	0.475	0.396	0.331	0.277	0.232	0.194	0.164
20	0.820	0.673	0.554	0.456	0.377	0.312	0.258	0.215	0.178	0.149

%	11	12	13	14	15	16	17	18	19	20
Period										
1	0.901	0.893	0.885	0.877	0.870	0.862	0.855	0.847	0.840	0.833
2	0.812	0.797	0.783	0.769	0.756	0.743	0.731	0.718	0.706	0.694
3	0.731	0.712	0.693	0.675	0.658	0.641	0.624	0.609	0.593	0.579
4	0.659	0.636	0.613	0.592	0.572	0.552	0.534	0.516	0.499	0.482
5	0.593	0.567	0.543	0.519	0.497	0.476	0.456	0.437	0.419	0.402
6	0.535	0.507	0.480	0.456	0.432	0.410	0.390	0.370	0.352	0.335
7	0.482	0.452	0.425	0.400	0.376	0.354	0.333	0.314	0.296	0.279
8	0.434	0.404	0.376	0.351	0.327	0.305	0.285	0.266	0.249	0.233
9	0.391	0.361	0.333	0.308	0.284	0.263	0.243	0.225	0.209	0.194
10	0.352	0.322	0.295	0.270	0.247	0.227	0.208	0.191	0.176	0.162
11	0.317	0.287	0.261	0.237	0.215	0.195	0.178	0.162	0.148	0.135
12	0.286	0.257	0.231	0.208	0.187	0.168	0.152	0.137	0.124	0.112
13	0.258	0.229	0.204	0.182	0.163	0.145	0.130	0.116	0.104	0.093
14	0.232	0.205	0.181	0.160	0.141	0.125	0.111	0.099	0.088	0.078
15	0.209	0.183	0.160	0.140	0.123	0.108	0.095	0.084	0.074	0.065
16	0.188	0.163	0.141	0.123	0.107	0.093	0.081	0.071	0.062	0.054
17	0.170	0.146	0.125	0.108	0.093	0.080	0.069	0.060	0.052	0.045
18	0.153	0.130	0.111	0.095	0.081	0.069	0.059	0.051	0.044	0.038
19	0.138	0.116	0.098	0.083	0.070	0.060	0.051	0.043	0.037	0.031
20	0.124	0.104	0.087	0.073	0.061	0.051	0.043	0.037	0.031	0.026

%	21	22	23	24	25	26	27	28	29	30
Period										
1	0.826	0.820	0.813	0.806	0.800	0.794	0.787	0.781	0.775	0.769
2	0.683	0.672	0.661	0.650	0.640	0.630	0.620	0.610	0.601	0.592
3	0.564	0.551	0.537	0.524	0.512	0.500	0.488	0.477	0.466	0.455
4	0.467	0.451	0.437	0.423	0.410	0.397	0.384	0.373	0.361	0.350
5	0.386	0.370	0.355	0.341	0.328	0.315	0.303	0.291	0.280	0.269
6	0.319	0.303	0.289	0.275	0.262	0.250	0.238	0.227	0.217	0.207
7	0.263	0.249	0.235	0.222	0.210	0.198	0.188	0.178	0.168	0.159
8	0.218	0.204	0.191	0.179	0.168	0.157	0.148	0.139	0.130	0.123
9	0.180	0.167	0.155	0.144	0.134	0.125	0.116	0.108	0.101	0.094
10	0.149	0.137	0.126	0.116	0.107	0.099	0.092	0.085	0.078	0.073
11	0.123	0.112	0.103	0.094	0.086	0.079	0.072	0.066	0.061	0.056
12	0.102	0.092	0.083	0.076	0.069	0.062	0.057	0.052	0.047	0.043
13	0.084	0.075	0.068	0.061	0.055	0.050	0.045	0.040	0.037	0.033
14	0.069	0.062	0.055	0.049	0.044	0.039	0.035	0.032	0.028	0.025
15	0.057	0.051	0.045	0.040	0.035	0.031	0.028	0.025	0.022	0.020
16	0.047	0.042	0.036	0.032	0.028	0.025	0.022	0.019	0.017	0.015
17	0.039	0.034	0.030	0.026	0.023	0.020	0.017	0.015	0.013	0.012
18	0.032	0.028	0.024	0.021	0.018	0.016	0.014	0.012	0.010	0.009
19	0.027	0.023	0.020	0.017	0.014	0.012	0.011	0.009	0.008	0.007
20	0.022	0.019	0.016	0.014	0.012	0.010	0.008	0.007	0.006	0.005

%	31	32	33	34	35	36	37	38	39	40
Period										
1	0.763	0.758	0.752	0.746	0.741	0.735	0.730	0.725	0.719	0.714
2	0.583	0.574	0.565	0.557	0.549	0.541	0.533	0.525	0.518	0.510
3	0.445	0.435	0.425	0.416	0.406	0.398	0.389	0.381	0.372	0.364
4	0.340	0.329	0.320	0.310	0.301	0.292	0.284	0.276	0.268	0.260
5	0.259	0.250	0.240	0.231	0.223	0.215	0.207	0.200	0.193	0.186
6	0.198	0.189	0.181	0.173	0.165	0.158	0.151	0.145	0.139	0.133
7	0.151	0.143	0.136	0.129	0.122	0.116	0.110	0.105	0.100	0.095
8	0.115	0.108	0.102	0.096	0.091	0.085	0.081	0.076	0.072	0.068
9	0.088	0.082	0.077	0.072	0.067	0.063	0.059	0.055	0.052	0.048
10	0.067	0.062	0.058	0.054	0.050	0.046	0.043	0.040	0.037	0.035
11	0.051	0.047	0.043	0.040	0.037	0.034	0.031	0.029	0.027	0.025
12	0.039	0.036	0.033	0.030	0.027	0.025	0.023	0.021	0.019	0.018
13	0.030	0.027	0.025	0.022	0.020	0.018	0.017	0.015	0.014	0.013
14	0.023	0.021	0.018	0.017	0.015	0.014	0.012	0.011	0.010	0.009
15	0.017	0.016	0.014	0.012	0.011	0.010	0.009	0.008	0.007	0.006
16	0.013	0.012	0.010	0.009	0.008	0.007	0.006	0.006	0.005	0.005
17	0.010	0.009	0.008	0.007	0.006	0.005	0.005	0.004	0.004	0.003
18	0.008	0.007	0.006	0.005	0.005	0.004	0.003	0.003	0.003	0.002
19	0.006	0.005	0.004	0.004	0.003	0.003	0.003	0.002	0.002	0.002
20	0.005	0.004	0.003	0.003	0.002	0.002	0.002	0.002	0.001	0.001

%	1	2	3	4	5	6	7	8	9	10
Period										
1	0.990	0.980	0.971	0.962	0.952	0.943	0.935	0.926	0.917	0.909
2	1.970	1.942	1.913	1.886	1.859	1.833	1.808	1.783	1.759	1.736
3	2.941	2.884	2.829	2.775	2.723	2.673	2.624	2.577	2.531	2.487
4	3.902	3.808	3.717	3.630	3.546	3.465	3.387	3.312	3.240	3.170
5	4.853	4.713	4.580	4.452	4.329	4.212	4.100	3.993	3.890	3.791
6	5.795	5.601	5.417	5.242	5.076	4.917	4.767	4.623	4.486	4.355
7	6.728	6.472	6.230	6.002	5.786	5.582	5.389	5.206	5.033	4.868
8	7.652	7.325	7.020	6.733	6.463	6.210	5.971	5.747	5.535	5.335
9	8.566	8.162	7.786	7.435	7.108	6.802	6.515	6.247	5.995	5.759
10	9.471	8.983	8.530	8.111	7.722	7.360	7.024	6.710	6.418	6.145
11	10.368	9.787	9.253	8.760	8.306	7.887	7.499	7.139	6.805	6.495
12	11.255	10.575	9.954	9.385	8.863	8.384	7.943	7.536	7.161	6.814
13	12.134	11.348	10.635	9.986	9.394	8.853	8.358	7.904	7.487	7.103
14	13.004	12.106	11.296	10.563	9.899	9.295	8.745	8.244	7.786	7.367
15	13.865	12.849	11.938	11.118	10.380	9.712	9.108	8.559	8.061	7.606
16	14.718	13.578	12.561	11.652	10.838	10.106	9.447	8.851	8.313	7.824
17	15.562	14.292	13.166	12.166	11.274	10.477	9.763	9.122	8.544	8.022
18	16.398	14.992	13.754	12.659	11.690	10.828	10.059	9.372	8.756	8.201
19	17.226	15.678	14.324	13.134	12.085	11.158	10.336	9.604	8.950	8.365
20	18.046	16.351	14.877	13.590	12.462	11.470	10.594	9.818	9.129	8.514

%	11	12	13	14	15	16	17	18	19	20
Period										
1	0.901	0.893	0.885	0.877	0.870	0.862	0.855	0.847	0.840	0.833
2	1.713	1.690	1.668	1.647	1.626	1.605	1.585	1.566	1.547	1.528
3	2.444	2.402	2.361	2.322	2.283	2.246	2.210	2.174	2.140	2.106
4	3.102	3.037	2.974	2.914	2.855	2.798	2.743	2.690	2.639	2.589
5	3.696	3.605	3.517	3.433	3.352	3.274	3.199	3.127	3.058	2.991
6	4.231	4.111	3.998	3.889	3.784	3.685	3.589	3.498	3.410	3.326
7	4.712	4.564	4.423	4.288	4.160	4.039	3.922	3.812	3.706	3.605
8	5.146	4.968	4.799	4.639	4.487	4.344	4.207	4.078	3.954	3.837
9	5.537	5.328	5.132	4.946	4.772	4.607	4.451	4.303	4.163	4.031
10	5.889	5.650	5.426	5.216	5.019	4.833	4.659	4.494	4.339	4.192
11	6.207	5.938	5.687	5.453	5.234	5.029	4.836	4.656	4.487	4.327
12	6.492	6.194	5.918	5.660	5.421	5.197	4.988	4.793	4.611	4.439
13	6.750	6.424	6.122	5.842	5.583	5.342	5.118	4.910	4.715	4.533
14	6.982	6.628	6.302	6.002	5.724	5.468	5.229	5.008	4.802	4.611
15	7.191	6.811	6.462	6.142	5.847	5.575	5.324	5.092	4.876	4.675
16	7.379	6.974	6.604	6.265	5.954	5.668	5.405	5.162	4.938	4.730
17	7.549	7.120	6.729	6.373	6.047	5.749	5.475	5.222	4.990	4.775
18	7.702	7.250	6.840	6.467	6.128	5.818	5.534	5.273	5.033	4.812
19	7.839	7.366	6.938	6.550	6.198	5.877	5.584	5.316	5.070	4.843
20	7.963	7.469	7.025	6.623	6.259	5.929	5.628	5.353	5.101	4.870

%	21	22	23	24	25	26	27	28	29	30
Period										
1	0.826	0.820	0.813	0.806	0.800	0.794	0.787	0.781	0.775	0.769
2	1.509	1.492	1.474	1.457	1.440	1.424	1.407	1.392	1.376	1.361
3	2.074	2.042	2.011	1.981	1.952	1.923	1.896	1.868	1.842	1.816
4	2.540	2.494	2.448	2.404	2.362	2.320	2.280	2.241	2.203	2.166
5	2.926	2.864	2.803	2.745	2.689	2.635	2.583	2.532	2.483	2.436
6	3.245	3.167	3.092	3.020	2.951	2.885	2.821	2.759	2.700	2.643
7	3.508	3.416	3.327	3.242	3.161	3.083	3.009	2.937	2.868	2.802
8	3.726	3.619	3.518	3.421	3.329	3.241	3.156	3.076	2.999	2.925
9	3.905	3.786	3.673	3.566	3.463	3.366	3.273	3.184	3.100	3.019
10	4.054	3.923	3.799	3.682	3.571	3.465	3.364	3.269	3.178	3.092
11	4.177	4.035	3.902	3.776	3.656	3.543	3.437	3.335	3.239	3.147
12	4.278	4.127	3.985	3.851	3.725	3.606	3.493	3.387	3.286	3.190
13	4.362	4.203	4.053	3.912	3.780	3.656	3.538	3.427	3.322	3.223
14	4.432	4.265	4.108	3.962	3.824	3.695	3.573	3.459	3.351	3.249
15	4.489	4.315	4.153	4.001	3.859	3.726	3.601	3.483	3.373	3.268
16	4.536	4.357	4.189	4.033	3.887	3.751	3.623	3.503	3.390	3.283
17	4.576	4.391	4.219	4.059	3.910	3.771	3.640	3.518	3.403	3.295
18	4.608	4.419	4.243	4.080	3.928	3.786	3.654	3.529	3.413	3.304
19	4.635	4.442	4.263	4.097	3.942	3.799	3.664	3.539	3.421	3.311
20	4.657	4.460	4.279	4.110	3.954	3.808	3.673	3.546	3.427	3.316

%	31	32	33	34	35	36	37	38	39	40
Period										
1	0.763	0.758	0.752	0.746	0.741	0.735	0.730	0.725	0.719	0.714
2	1.346	1.331	1.317	1.303	1.289	1.276	1.263	1.250	1.237	1.224
3	1.791	1.766	1.742	1.719	1.696	1.673	1.652	1.630	1.609	1.589
4	2.130	2.096	2.062	2.029	1.997	1.966	1.935	1.906	1.877	1.849
5	2.390	2.345	2.302	2.260	2.220	2.181	2.143	2.106	2.070	2.035
6	2.588	2.534	2.483	2.433	2.385	2.339	2.294	2.251	2.209	2.168
7	2.739	2.677	2.619	2.562	2.508	2.455	2.404	2.355	2.308	2.263
8	2.854	2.786	2.721	2.658	2.598	2.540	2.485	2.432	2.380	2.331
9	2.942	2.868	2.798	2.730	2.665	2.603	2.544	2.487	2.432	2.379
10	3.009	2.930	2.855	2.784	2.715	2.649	2.587	2.527	2.469	2.414
11	3.060	2.978	2.899	2.824	2.752	2.683	2.618	2.555	2.496	2.438
12	3.100	3.013	2.931	2.853	2.779	2.708	2.641	2.576	2.515	2.456
13	3.129	3.040	2.956	2.876	2.799	2.727	2.658	2.592	2.529	2.469
14	3.152	3.061	2.974	2.892	2.814	2.740	2.670	2.603	2.539	2.477
15	3.170	3.076	2.988	2.905	2.825	2.750	2.679	2.611	2.546	2.484
16	3.183	3.088	2.999	2.914	2.834	2.757	2.685	2.616	2.551	2.489
17	3.193	3.097	3.007	2.921	2.840	2.763	2.690	2.621	2.555	2.492
18	3.201	3.104	3.012	2.926	2.844	2.767	2.693	2.624	2.557	2.494
19	3.207	3.109	3.017	2.930	2.848	2.770	2.696	2.626	2.559	2.496
20	3.211	3.113	3.020	2.933	2.850	2.772	2.698	2.627	2.561	2.497

Glossary of terms

Accounting period

The period of time between two reporting dates.

Accounting policies

These are disclosed in the annual reports published by quoted companies and represent the interpretation of accounting principles and requirements adopted by the board of directors.

Accounting principles

A number of generally accepted accounting principles are used in preparing financial statements. They are only generally accepted and do not have the force of law. You should note that sometimes they are referred to as accounting concepts and conventions.

Accounting rate of return

A method used to evaluate an investment opportunity that ignores the time value of money. The return generated by an investment opportunity is expressed as a percentage of the capital outlay.

Acquisition

The process by which a company acquires a controlling interest in the voting shares of another company.

Amortisation

The writing-off of a fixed asset over a time period. It is often used in conjunction with intangible assets, e.g. goodwill. See depreciation.

Annual report

A report issued to shareholders and other interested parties which normally includes a chairman's statement, report of the directors, review of operations , financial statements and associated notes.

Annuity

A series of payments of an equal, or constant, amount of money at fixed intervals for a specified number of periods.

Arbitrage

The purchase of securities or commodities in one market for immediate resale in another in order to profit from the price difference.

Arbitrage Pricing Theory (APT)

The principle which underpins APT is that two assets that have identical risk characteristics must offer the same return or an arbitrage opportunity will exist. APT attempts to measure the various dimensions of market related risk in terms of several underlying economic factors, such as inflation, monthly production and interest rates, which systematically affect the price of all shares.

Architecture (distinctive capabilities)

A unique structure of relational contracts within, or around the firm. Firms may establish these relationships with and among their employees (internal architecture), with their suppliers or customers (external architecture), or among a group of firms engaged in related activities (networks).

Balance sheet

A statement showing the financial position of a company in terms of its assets and liabilities at a specified point in time.

Bank borrowings

Includes bank overdraft and bank loans.

Beta

A relative measure of volatility determined by comparing a share's returns to the market's returns. The greater the volatility, the higher the beta.

Business value

The value generated by the free cash flows in which *all* providers of funds have a claim.

Capital Asset Pricing Model (CAPM)

A statistical model developed in the mid-1960's, which is based upon the observation that some shares are more volatile than others. This means that when stock markets rise these shares rise faster and higher than the markets, and when the stock markets fall they fall faster and further. The return on any risky asset is the risk-free interest rate plus a risk premium which is a multiple of the beta and the premium on the market as a whole.

Capital investment appraisal

The evaluation of proposed capital projects. Sometimes referred to as project appraisal.

Capital structure

The composition of a company's sources of long-term funds e.g. equity and debt.

Cash flow "drivers"

Means by which free cash flow estimates can be generated and consist of:

1. Sales growth rate

2. Operating profit margin

3. Cash tax rate

4. Fixed capital investment

5. Working capital investment

Cash flow statement

A statement that UK and US companies are required to include in their published accounts. Such statements analyse cash flows under three types of activity:

Investing activities

Financial activities

Operating activities.

Compounding

A technique for determining a future value given a present value, a time period and an interest rate.

Continuing period

Time horizon beyond the planning period.

Corporate value

Where a business holds investments in other businesses, the benefits of which are not captured in the business valuation process, any such benefits have to be added to business value to determine corporate value.

Cost of capital

The cost of long-term funds to a company.

Creative accounting

The name given to a number of approaches by which companies could use (and have used) considerable judgement to produce results which put them in the best possible light, whilst staying within the letter of the law.

Creditors, amounts owing within one year

The amounts of money owed and payable by the business within one year, e.g. short-term loans.

Creditors, amounts owing after more than one year

Long-term loans and other liabilities payable after one year.

Critical value appraisal

A method of appraisal used to judge whether in financial terms any benefit might result from an organisational change. It requires the calculation of:

1. current market value

2. business value *as is*

3. business value with improvements.

Cross-sectional analysis

Method of estimating the cost of equity for an unquoted business entity. Cross-sectional models are also called "accounting" or "fundamental" models.

Current assets

Those assets of a company that are reasonably expected to be realised in cash, or sold, or consumed during the normal operating cycle of the business. They include stock, debtors, short term investments, bank and cash balances.

Current liabilities

Those liabilities which a company may rely upon to finance short-term activities. They include creditors, bank overdraft, proposed final dividend, and current taxation.

Current ratio

A measure of short-term solvency. It is calculated as current assets divided by current liabilities. It gives an indication of a company's ability to pay its way within one year.

Debentures

A written acknowledgement of a debt owing by a company. Normally the debt carries a fixed rate of interest and it is repayable within a specified number of years. The debt may be secured on certain of the company's assets, or it may be unsecured.

Debtors

Amounts owed to a company by its customers.

Depreciation

An accounting adjustment to take account of the diminution in value of a fixed asset over its economic life.

Discounted Cash Flow (DCF)

A technique for calculating whether a sum receivable at some time in the future is worthwhile in terms of value today. It involves discounting, or scaling-down, future cash flows.

Diversifiable risk

That part of total risk that can be eliminated in a diversified portfolio. (Also called unsystematic or specific risk).

Dividend

The proportion of the profits of a company distributed to shareholders.

Dividend cover

A ratio showing the number of times the dividend of a company is covered by earnings.

Dividend Valuation Model

A valuation model based upon the future dividend stream.

Dividend yield

A ratio showing the relationship between the ordinary dividend and the market price of an ordinary share.

Earnings per share

Profit before taxation divided by the weighted average number of ordinary shares in issue during the period. The calculation and result is shown by way of note in a company's annual report.

Efficient Markets Hypothesis

A hypothesis which postulates that there is no way to beat the stock market. Efficient means that share prices react quickly and unambiguously to new information.

Equity

The sum of issued share capital, capital reserves and revenue reserves which is also known as shareholders' funds, or net worth.

Equity risk premium

The excess return above the risk-free rate that investors demand for holding risky securities.

Equity share capital

The share capital of a company attributable to ordinary shareholders.

Financial risk

The risk that results from a significant dependency upon capital funded by debtt and which typically requires to be serviced by non-discretionary interest payments.

Fixed assets

Those assets which an organisation holds for use within the business and not for resale. They consist of tangible assets, like land and buildings, plant and machinery, vehicles, and fixtures and fittings; and intangible assets like goodwill.

Free cash flow

The cash available to the providers of finance.

Gearing

Expresses the relationship between some measure of interest-bearing capital and some measure of equity capital or the total capital employed.

Goodwill

The difference between the amount paid for a company as a whole and the net value of the assets and liabilities acquired.

Income statement

An US term for the profit and loss account.

Incremental Fixed Capital Investment (IFCI)

Investment in new assets to enable intended sales growth to occur.

Incremental Working Capital Investment (IWCI)

Investment in additional working capital, such as stocks of materials, to enable intended sales growth to occur.

Innovation (distinctive capabilities)

The ability to be innovative is a potential source of competitive advantage, although it may be difficult to sustain because of the potential for replication.

Intangible assets

Assets the value of which does not relate to their physical properties, e.g. goodwill and brands.

Internal rate of return (IRR)

The rate of discount at which the present value of the future cash flows is equal to the initial outlay, i.e. at the IRR the net present value is zero.

Interest payable

Money payable (but not necessary paid) on interest bearing debt.

Key ratio

A term sometimes given to the profitability ratio. In the UK this is usually defined as profit before tax plus interest payable expressed as a percentage of net capital employed.

Liabilities

The financial obligations owed by a company, these can be to shareholders, other providers of debt, trade creditors and other creditors.

Liquid assets

The difference between current assets and stock.

Liquid ratio

Liquid assets divided by current liabilities. It attempts to show a company's ability to pay its way in the short–term.

Loan capital

Finance that has been borrowed and not obtained from the shareholders.

Long-term liabilities

Liabilities which are not due for repayment within one year.

Market value of equity

The product of the market value of shares and the number of shares issued. Often referred to as market capitalisation.

MB ratio

The relationship between market value and shareholders' funds.

Net assets

See net capital employed.

Net capital employed

The sum of fixed assets, investments, current assets minus current liabilities.

Net current assets

See working capital.

Net present value (NPV)

The difference between the discounted value of future net cash inflows and the initial outlay.

Normalised free cash flow

Represents a situation where revenues generally reflect the continuation of the trends in the last forecast year adjusted to the midpoint of the business cycle. Operating costs should be based on sustainable margin levels and taxes should be based on the long-term expected rates.

Ordinary shares

Shares which attract the remaining profits after all other claims, and, in liquidation, which attract the remaining assets of a company after creditors and other charges have been satisfied.

Payback period

How long it will take to recover the outlay involved in a potential investment opportunity from net cash inflows.

Peer group analysis

An approach involving the analysis of peer group companies which can be used in conjunction with financial information relating to a company to estimate its value.

PE ratio

One of the most significant indicators of corporate performance which it is widely quoted in the financial press. It is calculated by dividing the market price of a share by the earnings per share (or the total market value by the total profit attributable to shareholders), i.e.

$$\text{PE ratio} = \frac{\text{Market price of a share}}{\text{Earnings per share}}$$

PE Relative

A means of comparing a company's PE ratio with the market as a whole:

$$\text{PE relative} = \frac{\text{PE of the company}}{\text{PE of the market}}$$

Perpetuity

A special case of an annuity in which the cash flows are assumed to be received in perpetuity.

Planning period

The period over which competitive advantage can be identified.

Portfolio Theory

A theory which suggests that an investor who diversifies will do better than one who does not.

Present Value Rule

A rule which explains why in a world of certainty accepting all projects with a positive NPV maximises the wealth of shareholders.

Profit and loss account

A statement showing what profit has been made over a period and the uses to which the profit has been put.

Quoted investments

Investments in another company which has its shares quoted on a stock exchange..

Reducing balance depreciation

A method of depreciation whereby the periodic amount written off is a percentage of the reduced balance. (cost less accummulated depreciation).

Relevant data

Relevant data for decision making is *future oriented* – that is *yet to be incurred*.

Replacement Fixed Capital Investment (RFCI)

Investment in fixed assets to maintain the level of productive facilities currently in place.

Reputation

A distinctive capability which enables a company to charge premium prices, or gain larger market share at a competitive price, for a functionally equivalent product.

Reserves – capital

That portion of total equity which is regarded as unavailable for withdrawal by proprietors, e.g. share premium and revaluation surplus.

Reserves – revenue (Profit and Loss Account)

That portion of total equity representing retained earnings which is available for withdrawal by proprietors.

Residual value

Value generated beyond the planning period.

Risk–free rate

The most secure return that can be achieved.

Sales (Turnover)

Income derived from the principal activities of a company, net of value added tax (VAT).

Sensitivity analysis

A commonly used approach to assessing risk whereby input variables are changed to determine their effect upon financial results.

Share capital (issued)

The product of the total number of shares issued and the nominal value of the shares.

Shareholder's funds

Another name for equity.

Shareholder value

A measure of value calculated as follows:

Business value

+   Marketable securities or investments

=   Corporate value

-    Market value of debt and obligations

=   Shareholder value

Shareholder Value Analysis

A valuation approach which considers in broad terms that the value of a business to a shareholder can be determined by discounting its future cash flows using an appropriate cost of capital.

Share premium

The excess paid for a share, to a company, over its nominal value.

Short-termism

A term associated with managing for today rather than tomorrow and beyond.

Straight line depreciation

A method of depreciation whereby an equal amount is written off the value of a fixed asset over its estimated economic life.

Strategic assets

These represent a source of competitive advantage by virtue of their dominance or market position.

Tangible assets

An asset having a physical identity such as land and buildings, plant and machinery, vehicles etc.

Time value of money

A concept which is an integral part of the discounted cash flow technique used in capital investment appraisal. It recognises that cash flows in the later years of an investment opportunity cannot be compared with cash flows in the earlier years.

Total assets

The sum of fixed assets, investments and current assets.

Value drivers

Determinants of future business value:

1. Sales growth rate

2. Operating profit margin

3. Cash tax rate

4. Fixed capital investment

5. Working capital investment

6. Planning period

7. Cost of capital.

Weighted Average Cost of Capital (WACC)

A term associated with the view that there is an optimal or ideal capital structure. It is calculated as follows:

$$\text{Weighted average cost of capital} = \%\text{Debt}(K_d) + \%\text{Equity}(K_e)$$

$$\text{where} \quad K_d = \text{Cost of debt}$$

$$K_e = \text{Cost of equity}$$

Working capital

The excess of current assets (stock, debtors and cash) over current liabilities (creditors, bank overdraft etc.).

Yield to redemption (maturity)

The percentage which equates all future cash flows and any redemption payment with current market value.

Index

Index, Author and Company